SWIMMING WITH CROCODILES

BY

RONN MOYER

Swimming with Crocodiles

Library of Congress Number: 2009901494
International Standard Book Number: 978-1-60126-167-0

Printed 2009 by

Masthof Press
219 Mill Road
Morgantown, PA 19543-9516

TABLE OF CONTENTS

ACKNOWLEDGEMENTS
AND DISCLAIMER

Working mostly through memory and recall, I was appreciative of the encouragement and assistance of Charles Bieber who proofed the manuscript and made various suggestions. Charles is a retired missionary, now approaching his 90th birthday, but still able to find my split infinitives and occasional misspells. I had the privilege of working with him in the office in Nigeria during my stay there in the fifties.

Also, my wife Diane has been patient and supportive during the hours I spent on the computer for which I am grateful. I received affirmation from our daughter Danielle, early in the process, which was also helpful.

Trying to be accurate and specific about events, which happened over fifty years ago, can present some challenges in recall. Wherein I may have made errors with names or events that happened back then, I apologize. My intent throughout has been to be as accurate as possible and to assure the reader that the book is definitely non-fiction.

The Brethren Volunteer Service program continues today after 60 years of sending volunteers all over this country and to many foreign countries. I'm thankful to them for online information to verify accuracy of dates and names. More than any other person or event, I am thankful to the Holy Spirit for inspiration to follow Jesus' teachings. It was all-important during my experiences in Nigeria and continues to this date. I hope you will draw meaning and inspiration from reading it.

PREFACE

In retrospect, it seems to me that some of the very biggest "life decisions" are made by youth—especially teens. In many instances these life decisions are forced on youth by our societal mores. Decisions regarding educational paths, vocations, life partners, alcohol/tobacco/drugs and choosing friends are a few. Of more importance is a decision to know and follow God and to lead a Christian life dedicated to following Jesus and the Bible.

An important decision regarding possible military service or alternative service can also determine a life-changing event. Some of us who are older faced conscription when such a decision was forced upon us as we passed age eighteen. Youth during those times were greatly influenced by their parents' teachings and that of their church denomination's stance. The "peace churches"— mainly the Church of the Brethren, Mennonite and Quaker—were strong on teaching the peace path of non-resistance as understood from the New Testament teachings and the example of Jesus. "Do not kill; Love your neighbor; Pray for those who despitefully use you, etc. etc.," were common teachings heard week after week in worship services.

Many of the youth from these denominations searched their consciences and belief systems and chose to do service in alternative fields such as hospital work, government construction, mental hospitals, inner city teaching and soup kitchens or going to foreign countries to rebuild war-torn infrastructure and assist in educating the youth. They agreed that they could do "something useful and helpful" for similar time periods to those serving in the military—typically 2-3 years duration.

Their peers and their communities, for trying to "take the easy road" or trying to "avoid their duty" often ridiculed these conscientious objectors. In reality, these projects for alternative service were often just as difficult and even dangerous but the majority of these men felt their duty was to try to assist and help people—not to pick up a firearm and kill people.

My personal privilege was to spend 2 ½ years in Nigeria, West Africa, teaching English to fifth graders, operating a large citrus orchard to supply missionaries fresh fruit for better diet and teaching students how to improve their agricultural methods to better feed their families. Conditions were sometimes severe. Typical temperatures ranged from 70 to 120 degrees in the shade; no indoor plumbing plus contaminated water supplies which had to be boiled and filtered; no telephones or computers; letters through the mail to the states took about one month to send and receive; no social life or night life opportunities and malaria on two occasions, were some of the downside.

This was no easy period of time—to say the least—yet it was the most meaningful and rewarding period of my life. When I finally came back home I understood that I had been an important asset in assisting students and families from Nigeria to get guidance and training to begin their lives on the right track. Years later, letters of thanks arrived at my home. Hindsight has convinced me that, even without my conscious knowledge, God was leading me through that time as a way of giving me confidence, spiritual strength and training for the work of my life to follow. I hope you will find it interesting to revisit these experiences with me as I reminisce in the following chapters and pages.

The purpose of this book is basically twofold. My hope is to uplift and advertise the program of Brethren Voluntary Service with a goal of encouraging today's youth, or older volunteers, to give a period of their lives to serve others less fortunate than themselves. The other purpose is to share with my progeny and friends, a very meaningful period of my life so that they can appreciate the adventure and the service given.

Perhaps YOU are one who is needed. Your contribution of time and talent could make a huge difference.

Additional information on the BVS program opportunities is available by email at bvs_gb@brethren.org or by calling toll free 1-800-323-8039.

FOREWORD

As assistant to the field secretary (executive) of the Church of the Brethren Mission in Nigeria from 1954 to 1960, with special assignment for personnel, I was privileged to come to know eight different Brethren Volunteer Service men who were assigned to Nigeria. Add to that the fact that my brother-in-law, my son, and my daughter-in-law also entered BVS later on, and you will understand why I have been so enthusiastic for BVS.

BVS-ers in Nigeria had not been recruited for particular assignments. When their conscientious objection to participation in military service was recognized, service in Nigeria was recognized as meeting the requirement that they give community service. It varied widely, from teaching, architectural planning, building, secretarial and administrative responsibilities, motor and equipment maintenance, to transportation (on unpredictable Nigeria roads), etc.

I did not need to be convinced, but I rapidly became aware of the important values of BVS. It provides opportunity to be "among you as one who serves" for hundreds of young men—and later, women. Unexpected assignments have often led to the honing of personal skills or, just as often, the discovery of unknown skills. (It is not unusual, I believe, for missionaries to discover they are using skills they did not know they had!) The effect of the service frequently led to the solidifying of career choices or, just as often, to a complete change in career choices.

In addition to actual assignments, the volunteers also have found broad educational opportunities in countries and societies different from their own. Besides, the tasks that they undertake make it possible for programs to be developed or carried forth with equal commitment and efficiency at less expense.

The detailed and very readable and informative descriptions, which Ronn Moyer provides in this book, are an important report of his own experience and growth, and are also a strong suggestion of what could happen to any volunteer. Ronn's descriptions of missionary life, environment, and relationship with national Nigerians is, I believe, one of the best such descriptions in print. I commend it to your reading, at the same time that I recommend Brethren Volunteer Service as an opportunity for you.

- Charles M. Bieber, M.Div., R.N.

INTRODUCTION

The time in history in which this story takes place essentially began following the end of the Korean War in 1953. The Korean conflict happened just five years after the end of World War II, and for young men just finishing high school in our country these years were critical decision making times. Since conscription was still the law of the land, young men were forced at the age of 18 to register with the U.S. Government for possible military service. During those years, females were not obligated to register or serve in the armed forces.

Representatives of the various armed forces were meeting high school students while still in school to try to convince them to register and join their particular branch of service. These included the U.S. Army, the Marine Corps, the Air Force, the Navy and the Coast Guard. Most young men enlisted in one of these service groups. Some of those registering were found to have physical problems or limitations, which would exempt them from being required to serve. Many of these exemptions were obvious but most were determined following the mandated "Army Physical," which was required of each man after registering at 18.

Fortunately, for many young men who were brought up in the more conservative church denominations, there existed the opportunity to apply for conscientious objector status. Men, who were approved for this exemption to military type services, were required to perform other types of humanitarian work in projects and places, which were approved by our government, in lieu of the military. The denominations, which were recognized as the "peace" churches and who had always taught that war is wrong and that killing people for any reason is wrong, were the Church of the Brethren, the Mennonites and the Quakers. It was also possible to be approved as a conscientious objector if from any other denomination but the prospects of being approved were much more difficult. Even for the "peace churches" young men were tested and had to write a letter about their specific beliefs and appear before a panel to verify their sincerity as well as provide various references from their pastors or laypersons that knew the young man who was applying for CO status.

Another alternative to active military service was non-combatant service like driving ambulances for wounded, assisting medics and kitchen duties for combat personnel, etc. The peace churches mostly taught that this was better than being put into a position to have to kill another, however history showed that many of these "non-combatant" personnel, in the heat of battle, had rifles shoved into their hands, and were thrust into the front lines when things got serious—against their will. Some of these men were killed without their rifles being fired.

For the purposes of this book, the focus will be on that group of young men who chose alternative service to the military. The types of service approved by our government as alternative service included a myriad of choices which again is a reflection of our government and their fairness and willingness to consider the plight of all those who were being drafted. Some men worked in dairy testing programs which supplied services to the military; some worked in mental hospitals as orderlies; others worked on farm projects which provided foodstuffs to the military; many were sent to other countries to perform rebuilding in war-ravaged countries and some went to teach in the school systems of other countries and cultures.

In many of these service projects, the amount of goodwill and help to poor, hungry and disadvantaged persons was a huge humanitarian service and was a fit for the young men who had been taught all their lives that they must not kill another human being no matter what the reasons. Many of these men in alternative service spent two plus years without ever being able to visit their families and without any vacation time. Their contributions were not only commendable but also difficult.

One of the programs, which caught the eye of the government, was called BVS. This stood for Brethren Volunteer Service. This program was initiated in the late 1940s following WWII. It is a program of the Church of the Brethren, headquartered in Elgin, Illinois. The Mennonite and Quaker denominations also had similar programs for their men in alternative service. BVS then and now in 2008 continues to train not only young men but also young women to give at least one year of their lives in volunteer service. In more recent years there are also training units for middle age and older adults who similarly wish to serve those with needs.

The Peace Corps, under government auspices, was patterned after the BVS program after they learned about its successes during the first decade of its existence. Most of the work projects in the BVS program are spread within the confines of the states, but also a number are in foreign countries. Countries receiving Brethren Volunteer Service personnel during the interim since inception include Austria, Germany, Ireland, Serbia, Nigeria, Puerto Rico, Guatemala and many others.

Volunteer projects within the states are mostly for one year duration, although many of these service worker volunteers have stayed on their projects for two years or even longer. The foreign projects require a two-year commitment. Some criteria for assignment in foreign projects would usually expect a college graduate person as opposed to one just graduating from high school. Many enrollees into the BVS program are persons who have just finished high school and wish to do this before college. Some have gone to college for one or two years and then interrupt their education to enroll, while some wait until after graduation.

Indeed, the testimony of many of those persons has been that their year or more in service aided them in choosing a career and also choosing a college path in which to major. Without exception, BVSers, upon completion of their various projects, have evaluated their experience as life changing for the better and one of the most memorable times of their lives. Seldom are we challenged to give a meaningful portion of our lives to help and assist other persons who stand in need of assistance in one way or another.

CHAPTER 1

FACING CONSCRIPTION

The time was July 1953. I had just celebrated my eighteenth birthday and I was now required by law to register with the U.S. Government and become classified for service eligibility and availability for either the military or an alternative to the military services.

It was a scary time for each male youth. It felt as though I was signing my life over to some other power to manage as they decided, instead of as I would decide. At that time in history, females were not required to register or serve. It was a time of self-examination. Does my conscience tell me to join a branch of the military or does it dictate that I choose an alternate type of service? My peers from high school exerted pressure to conform to the majority with comments of "loyalty to country" and "join your school chums." Some had made decisions to enlist before being drafted so they might get preferential choice in the Navy, the Marines, the Air Force or the Coast Guard. They believed that if they waited to be drafted they would be placed in the Army even if that were not their choice. Representatives of the various branches of the armed forces were even brought into the high schools to try to convince each of us to join their service branch.

I was born and brought up in the Indian Creek Church of the Brethren. As a member there, I was taught the denomination's peace stance and strongly discouraged from considering any type of military service. Many of the members from our congregation had already been in alternative types of service due to their beliefs and conscience. In the forties, during World War II, some of our men went into Civilian Public Service (CPS). These men were assigned to work in public and state facilities in lieu of military service.

During the Korean War in the early fifties, a few joined the Air Force and Marines. Many others responded by conscience and the teachings of the church by applying as conscientious objectors for a 1-W status and served in state related institutions. During this interim between WWII and the Korean conflict, the Brethren Volunteer Service program commenced and some of the young men—and indeed some of the young women in our congregation—signed up to join BVS for a one or two year commitment. The BVS program opened projects across the states and also in many foreign countries.

Within the states, BVSers were assigned to projects such as retirement communities, hospitals, teaching among the Navajo Indians, farm work in Texas on state farm projects, or being normal control patients (or guinea pigs as they were referred to then) in experimental hospitals and medical facilities such as the National Institutes of Health (NIH). On foreign projects much time was spent by BVSers in Europe rebuilding schools and war-damaged buildings and other structures. Projects in Puerto Rico and Nigeria, West Africa, became available to assist missionaries in those areas. Over time, such foreign projects were open only to college graduates, but during my experience in the mid-fifties, high school graduates were also utilized—mostly with excellent results.

Now it was my time to make a life-changing decision. Most youth at eighteen and finished with high school, believe they have all the answers and that even our parents have inferior information and knowledge. In retrospect I can now see how little I knew of making life decisions and of understanding world affairs. We had lived a somewhat sheltered life to that point. As I considered the internal conscience messages I was receiving through my prayers and conversations with parents and counselors, it became clear to me that, if I was being required to "do something," it would be best to do something that would help those less fortunate than myself.

My training during formative years had always emphasized that it is right to follow biblical teachings such as, do not kill another human, love your enemies, do good to those who may hate you and pray for those who despitefully use you. I knew I had to choose alternative service to the military. The fact that there was no war or international conflict at that time was also a minor consideration. While there were other types of alternative service, sponsored and approved by the government, I strongly leaned in the direction of becoming a Brethren Volunteer Service worker.

The next test of will was to convince the draft board that I was sincere in my decision and that I was not merely trying to avoid military training but to initiate and hopefully receive the classification of 1-O (this, again was the classification for conscientious objectors). To do this required filing a petition to be classified as a CO which included writing a paper outlining my beliefs, reasons for request, proof of my stance, church affiliation and a list of persons as references to verify my sincerity. The next step required standing (literally) in front of a committee of the draft board and answering their tough questions. Most of the members on this committee obviously had no sympathy for an alternate stance to the military. They were required only to recognize that the government had approved this as a possibility to those genuinely committed to a peace position.

Before the draft board would approve my application and issue me a 1-O classification, two more hurdles had to be overcome. These were a written examination to determine one's basic intelligence quotient, and a physical examination—known to many as the dreaded "Army Physical." The written examination was given first and included 100 questions. I found the test to be much more elementary than I expected and I quickly became less apprehensive as the test progressed. It was a timed test and I completed the questions with answers before the time was up.

I took my test forward and handed it to the sergeant at the desk as we had been instructed to do and sat back down to await the time clock signal. There were approximately 40 of us taking the test as I recall, and we were all required to sit and wait as a battery of officers checked our tests, graded them and handed them back to us to take with us as we had our physical exam. When my test was returned and I had a 96 grade out of 100, I was not surprised since the test seemed to be quite easy. Soon thereafter as I stood in line with the other men awaiting the beginning of our physical exam, I overheard three of them in front of me sharing their results with each other. I could not believe what I heard when the one with the highest grade was a 61 and the other two in the 50s.

When one of them turned around and asked me what I got, for the first time I could remember, I was embarrassed to tell them because I felt sorry for them and didn't want them to reject me as "brain." I reluctantly turned over my paper and showed them my grade. They had a few raised eyebrows among them and turned away from me to continue their conversations, effectively cutting me off from any further dialogue.

I'll not mention all of the details of the physical examination other than to say that it was all of what you may have heard about the infamous Army physicals. Just a couple interesting remembrances of that day—as I was waiting in line to have my blood pressure taken at a desk manned by a short, redheaded sergeant, I was attracted by the shouting of the man. It seemed that as each of us approached his desk, he found something being done wrong and was yelling at each of us to "put your paper down here;" "sit facing forward;" "place you right elbow on my desk so I can attach to blood pressure cuff." He was obviously trying to intimidate each of us, exhibit his superiority and introduce us to life in the military. I became interested in just what it was he wanted and how he was saying each of us should present ourselves when it became our turn. Finally, after yelling at the fellow in front of me and giving him his papers to move on it was my turn.

I stepped forward and placed my papers in front of him as it seemed he was requesting, I turned facing away from him, sat on the chair and placed my arm on his desk as I thought he was desiring and waited. He said nothing for about ten seconds. I did not look at him but just sat there waiting. Finally he said with a loud voice, "You're the first G...D... guy to get this right all day long." He then took my blood pressure and handed me my papers. I stood up, thanked him and moved to the next station. I had other parts of my anatomy probed and examined and finally ended up at the desk of a captain representing the last stop in the process.

It should also be noted that the entire hour of the physical was done while all we had to wear was our undershorts. When my turn came and I stood in front of the officer, I handed him my papers including written tests and physical approvals. He proceeded to study my test results and finally looked up at me and said, "Mr. Moyer, you have scored extremely well on your tests. I would like to encourage you to consider going directly into officer's training school. You would be able to avoid much of the basic training others will be required to take."

My forms had been stamped in rather large letters with a rubber stamp, which printed 1-O on the cover sheet. (This meant that I was not planning to enter the military but was seeking alternative service.) I did not answer his suggestion of officer's school, but merely pointed to the 1-O designation. He paused, then said, "Oh yeah, well good luck" and initialed and handed my papers back to me. It was clear to me that he knew this was my position but hoped to persuade me otherwise to test my resolve by issuing a tempting offer.

A component of the test was to determine if there was a physical impediment that would defer a draftee into a 4-F classification. If such a classification as this was received, meaning the person was physically unfit to serve in the military, then that person would also not be required to serve in alternative service but could if they desired, and if they were able to perform adequately there. My having passed these tests mandated that I proceed with arranging a plan to do approved alternative service. At this point, Brethren Volunteer Service became my clear choice and I began the application processes soon thereafter.

CHAPTER 2

CHOOSING BRETHREN
VOLUNTEER SERVICE

I submitted my application to enter the next BVS Unit for March of 1955. Over a period of the next few weeks I was contacted for additional information and the references I included were contacted. I was finally approved and informed that I should report to the training center at New Winsdor, Maryland, the first of March. New apprehensions arose in that this was a totally new arena and I would be learning to know and interact with other youth, none of whom I knew.

The Brethren Volunteer Service Program, now some 60 years old, is still very active and continues to send out for service, not only youth, but now also middle-aged and senior adults. The number of project locations in which service projects are available include 35 projects in 19 different foreign countries and 87 projects in 23 different states domestically. Various sites have been used and continue to be used as locations to train the volunteers. The most recent units trained at this writing have been located in Florida and New Windsor (May '08) and three more are planned this year in July, in August and in September. The 2009 schedule lists five more training unit dates. Since its inception, there have been 279 different units trained and sent into the projects during the past 60 years.

Way back in 1955, my unit was number 26 and it was one of the smaller units with just eighteen members. We had two on-site trainers and a different guest teacher each week for the duration of the three months in training. The length of the training units currently is much shorter and usually is completed in two to three weeks. I remember that two of the guest teachers we had for a week each were Milton Hershey and Dan West, known internationally as the originator of Heifer Project.

It should be noted that while the service we were able to perform on these various projects was appreciated and in many cases a God-send, the motivation definitely stemmed from the law of conscription to the military. It is almost certain that few if any of us fellows would have spent two years away from home in this capacity except that we were obligated to some sort of service to humankind. An oversimplification would be to say that I experienced what I did due to God's intervening hand through the draft laws. In retrospect, however, I feel strongly that was the case.

It was and became the impetus to engage in vocation and life's work that would benefit others in need and would cause me to be a conduit through which the Lord's work could be accomplished. At the time it was happening I did not realize my fit in God's plans. Now, however, I look back and can see how I was trained for continuing work in service areas in spite of myself and my many failures and weaknesses.

My point in sharing these experiences is that even though I was obligated to make a choice and to do "something," the end result proved to be a highlight of my youth and indeed my life. The two and one-half years from start to finish of my particular project was the most meaningful, life-changing and memorable period of my life. Therefore, I conclude, I would strongly encourage anyone of any age—especially post high school youth—to consider "giving one or possibly two years" of their lives in similar project experience. They would be making a life-changing decision for the better without the coercion of a military draft and I believe it would be even more meaningful than those of us who felt forced. During the fifties and during conscription there was a third choice. For refusing to do either military service or alternative service one faced imprisonment. A significant number of young men experienced that outcome and some of them were really used by God within the prison system to benefit other men in their rehabilitation.

Getting back to the progression of the story, I packed clothes and personal items, intending to spend the next two years away from home. Thankfully the BVS program offered each of us guidelines to know what to pack and how much of it would be needed. The training site back then was the Brethren Service Center in New Windsor, Maryland.

During that post WWII period, the Church of the Brethren was active in collecting used clothing and blankets to send to countries around the world which had been war ravaged or were poor through destruction and famines, etc. Two large tractor-trailer trucks were continually on the road from the New Windsor base to congregations of the Church of the Brethren over a large geographical radius. People in the congregations would collect serviceable used clothing from members and friends, pack them in boxes and bags and await the truck on a regular schedule.

New Windsor Service Center was a former college campus purchased by the denomination to use as a retreat center and processing center to collect, package and distribute clothing and blankets worldwide. Its dormitories and offices were refurbished and now accommodate large groups for overnight conventions and meetings as well as training facilities for BVS.

In the fifties, as previously mentioned, the training units were of longer duration—in our case three months. This, however, was somewhat misleading because the actual training was confined to the mornings, while after lunch we went from the classroom to the processing center and proceeded to sort, package and bale clothing for distribution. In this regard we were combining training time with project time, since the processing center was in fact the project for some of the BVSers who chose it or may have been unqualified for other projects.

Evenings included events such as planned campfires and devotions and weekends included being bussed to nearby congregations for worship services. Trips were also arranged to tour Washington, D.C. and for a few days we bussed to Baltimore and worked in depressed areas doing cleanup and painting work. These experiences helped the directors of the unit observe each of our talents and us so that they could recommend appropriate units for service after training. How we were able to work together or had conflicts and how we resolved them also came into focus.

The processing of clothing at the service center soon became quite boring for all of us and we began looking eagerly to beginning our projects. I was especially fortunate when one day while sorting and baling clothes, the phone rang and I was summoned to the phone. I immediately suspected an emergency back home since I didn't believe anyone else would call. It turned out to be the Director of the Center in the main office complex—a man named John Eberly. He said, "Ronn, I see from your application that you have had training in shorthand." I acknowledged that I had one year of shorthand in high school but that was three years ago and I had not used it since. He said, "That's OK, drop what you are doing and come up to my office. I have some letters to dictate to you." I said, "I'll be there soon." After all, this was the big boss calling.

On my way there I began "shaking in my boots." I had never taken dictation per se and had forgotten many of the brief forms and more than I had learned. I explained this to him, but he smiled and said, "Let's give it a try and I'll go slowly." What a fiasco, I had to return to his office twice to ask him what he said since I could not read my own shorthand. Well, fortunately he was patient and I continued to do office work throughout the balance of the three months instead of the "boring" clothing processing. I was also the envy of others in my unit. Later during that period I also did office work for Roy Hiteshew, the business administrator.

The training proceeded week after week and the effect of working with each other every day in close proximity naturally caused us to become very close with each other in sharing work, eating, prayer, problems, aspirations and allowing our personalities to blossom forth with each other. Many lasting friendships happened during our training and letters continued after training from our projects to those of our fellow unit members in their projects. As we were approaching the end of training, booklets were distributed to each of us, listing all the projects currently open and encouraging each of us to study the manual and list our choice of projects if approved, with a first, second and third choice.

During the latter days of the training, we went by our trusty bus to Camp Swatara for our personal evaluations. This was a somewhat intense time where we were asked to evaluate each other along with guidance from our unit leaders. One of the procedures was to place eighteen chairs in a circle and one chair in the center of the circle. One at a time, we sat in the middle while our fellow BVSers—starting around the circle told us what our faults and weaknesses were and what they viewed as our strengths. During this time of evaluation, the person in the center being evaluated was not allowed to speak and was instructed to listen closely to each criticism and compliment without rebuttal or judgment. Each participant agreed to be as loving and as honest as possible. While it was difficult to accept each person's opinions without commenting, it certainly was a growing experience and was done in love and concern for each person and their future project wherever that would be.

I learned that a project at the Brethren Hospital in Castener, Puerto Rico, was in need of a handy man and listed this as my first choice. I was interviewed for that project and the coordinators of our unit told me that they thought I would be a good fit. They reasoned that even though I did not yet have college training and experience, I was nearly 20 years old and had maturity. I was encouraged to begin learning Spanish immediately so as to make an easier transition to that project. A couple weeks went by and I was studying Spanish as I had time, when I was summoned to the training area one day near the end of the scheduled training unit. I was told that the project in Puerto Rico was no longer open and would I be interested in going to Nigeria, West Africa, instead.

Since my first preference was simply to do a project in a foreign country, to travel and gain experience in other cultures, I nearly jumped at the suggestion and opportunity. The job description in Nigeria was to assist H. Stover Kulp (who was the first missionary of the Church of the Brethren to Nigeria in 1924) as Administrative Assistant in the central headquarters at Garkida. I learned that the need to obtain a passport and visa to Nigeria would take a couple of months, which would end up extending my total tour of duty to 2 ½ years. I was excited about the prospects and adventure ahead.

CHAPTER 3

INTERIM PROJECT AT NATIONAL INSTITUTES OF HEALTH

My BVS training was completed in June of '55 and my assignment to Garkida, Nigeria, West Africa, was confirmed. Now, however, the program had to help me find an interim project stateside because I needed to procure visas, a passport and clothing for tropical weather for a two-year period. It would also be necessary to be inoculated with as many as six different serums for the various medical dangers to be encountered in the tropics where civilization is quite primitive. I would also need to begin malaria medications prior to my arrival in Nigeria to build up a resistance to this prevalent disease carried by their common mosquito.

As it turned out, another young fellow from our unit was also assigned to Garkida to teach in the primary schools there. His name was Curt Weddle and he was from the midwest, but had already completed two years at Elizabethtown College and was engaged to another student he met there. The relationship would have to wait until his return, but it did give me opportunity to plan with him and travel with him so that neither of us would need to make the journey alone.

During the wait to obtain the necessary papers and arrange the detail of our trip, I was able to arrange to work on a

13

project at the National Institutes of Health in Bethesda, Maryland. Bethesda is a suburb of Washington, D.C. Some of the youth from our unit were also going there for a short term as they prepared for their permanent projects. This gave us opportunity for some social life on weekends while we waited. During this time I was assigned to the fourth floor "mental unit" and soon learned that already three other youth from the Mennonite Voluntary Service were working on that floor. These two young women and another fellow became quick friends and we were able to visit some local sites and attend a few concerts in the area. We were called "normal control patients" and some folks referred to us as "guinea pigs" since many tests were performed using us as experimental subjects.

The program into which I was directed was doing mostly experiments using various drugs and was especially interested in the treatment of schizophrenic patients. There was a rather strong belief in the mid fifties that the drug lysergic acid—better known as LSD—would be useful in the treatment of schizophrenics. LSD was used in the study of schizophrenia and other mental disorders and as a psychedelic drug in a psychotic state. When under the influence, one experiences many different illusions.

Some of the illusions that I experienced were persons' shape changes like their heads would be disproportionately large while the body was small and their eyes would appear big, then small and the closest example of this might be the crazy mirrors one finds in carnivals and the house of mirrors. Besides sight variations there were physical oddities. We were required to give urine samples under the influence and under normal situations for comparison purposes. The problem was that when I was under LSD, my brain was not able to send the signals to the bladder to initiate urination. When I was eating, I could chew but didn't know how to swallow. When I walked down the corridor, the walls would close in then expand out—then they would tilt from one side to another so that I would put my hands out to prevent myself from falling.

Psychologically, I was constantly certain that people were watching me and laughing at me. I did not like that feeling and tried hard to behave normally. I found I could force myself to act normal for a few minutes at a time through concentration but would soon slide back under the influence. Of approximately a dozen times I had the drug administered, most were by injection intravenously, so that within ten seconds, I could taste a metallic taste on my tongue and within only a few minutes I was totally under the influence. Other times the medication was given orally and it would take about 20 minutes to a half hour to be fully involved.

In retrospect, I realize that I could not understand why anyone would continually take the drug for hallucinatory purposes because the more often I had LSD injected into my system, the more nauseous I became. The testing done by NIH however, had precautions and controls, which were not available or used in the illicit market some years later. Our body weight, age and gender were considered when the drug was administered. It was not until some years later that LSD was available for drug users through illegal channels and I presume it is still available in the illicit market if one desires.

In my situation the testing went as follows: First I was given a series of dexterity tests under normal conditions. These were all tabulated and graded. Then I was given the LSD intravenously and about fifteen minutes later, after it had really taken effect, I was again required to take the same dexterity tests while under the influence, and comparisons were made between the two. I was then fed a meal, with other staff observing my abilities or inabilities. Then I was required to give a urine sample for testing. Following that I was allowed to sleep. I always wanted to go to sleep—mostly because I was really sleepy from the experience and secondly to be away from people—probably because of the embarrassment concern.

When I was judged "back to normal" I was summoned by one of the psychiatrists and we would have about a half-hour session of his asking me all kinds of questions and me sharing the fantasies I had. He even encouraged me to try to analyze myself: Why I felt like I did; was it related to childhood experiences; was I anxious; was I nauseous; and many other questions. I found this part of the testing very interesting and always looked forward to talking with the shrink.

Some of the other BVSers from our unit were on the seventh floor on salt free diet tests and water retention tests. Those on salt free diets for more than a week really became somewhat sick. They had spells of vomiting and tried to avoid food but were required to continue through their discomfort. A couple of those on water retention tests were required to begin at 8 a.m. with 100cc of water and every half hour drink another glass of water but were not permitted to void until after lunch time. They would lie in their beds on their backs and moan for relief. We would sometimes visit them and make them laugh. It was not a nice thing to do but it was fun at the time.

Being healthy youth, we looked for times to have fun and play pranks. The first thing which would happen, most mornings around 7:30 a.m., one of the African American orderlies would enter our room (double room with a Mennonite fellow and myself as patients), and pleasantly say, "Good morning fellas, time to wake up and get ready for breakfast." He would then slip a thermometer into our mouths, leave the room and return in about five minutes to retrieve the thermometer and chart our temps and ask us if we voted. (When asked if we voted today, it meant "Did you have a bowel movement today" yes or no.)

One morning, my roommate, Dale, and I agreed to play a trick on the orderly whose name was Grady. After slipping the thermometer in my mouth and leaving the room, I pulled it out and waved a lighter under it until it reached 106 degrees, then reinserted it and waited. Grady came whistling back into the room, pulled the thermometer as I feigned sleep. He looked at it, blinked, and then looked again while I was peeking. His eyes got big like saucers and he said to me, "MAN, YOU IS SICK!!!" Both Dale and I nearly rolled out of our beds laughing at his expense. Soon Grady was laughing louder than we were. We had a real good relationship with both the nurses and orderlies during that time.

Another time, Dale and I were back to our rooms before the Mennonite girls in the adjacent double room came back for the evening. We thought it might be fun to hide under their beds when they came in to listen to what they talk about and with a prearranged signal, we would both push up on their beds and yell. The beds were Hollywood beds with spreads that reached the floor and bolsters on top to affect a sofa appearance and function during the day. We were not waiting long when they arrived and one of them immediately plopped down on the bed under which I was lying and the springs came down hitting me in the gut. I almost grunted but held quietly.

Soon we saw shoes drop down, and then stockings hit the floor. Whoa!! We decided without talking that we best not wait longer since they were beginning to undress. So we signaled, pushed up under them and yelled. I haven't heard shrill screaming like that since. Nurses came running and an orderly. Fortunately, everyone was able to have a laugh, including the staff. There was only one patient on the floor and Ginny was sleeping some distance away. The girls threatened to get even, but it never happened.

CHAPTER 4

THE JOURNEY TO WEST AFRICA

Nearly six months after the beginning of the training unit commenced, we finally had all of our inoculations, our passports and visas in hand and a travel guide from headquarters in Elgin, Illinois—the central office location at that time for the Church of the Brethren. The tickets for our train ride showed us embarking at Philadelphia and traveling due north through the New England States, crossing the St. Lawrence River into Canada and ending the train ride in Quebec, Canada. Since my home was almost directly between New Windsor and Philadelphia, my family made arrangements to pick us up at the training center, stay overnight at my home and then deliver us to the train terminal to begin our long trip. The journey to Quebec was unremarkable, but the rest of the trip was challenging and even scary at times.

We spent two days in Quebec to make connections with the ocean liner, which would take us to France and England. When we located the terminal along the St. Lawrence River, we finally found the ship on which we had reservations. It was emblazoned on the bow with its name, "FRANCONIA." I found this ironic since I spent my formative years in elementary school in the Franconia Elementary School in a small town of Franconia near my home. The vessel was a British ship and the name probably came from that part of West Germany where a much older Franconia exists.

This ship seemed extremely large to both Curt and me, but we had never before been on an ocean-going passenger ship. By today's standards, it was in fact a rather small ship and my recollection is that it did not have the amenities one would experience on today's cruise ships. When we found our stateroom, we noted that there were three beds in it, without toilet facilities. It turned out that the third bed was assigned to George, a furrier, going from Canada to Europe on vacation. George was a man about 60 years of age and quite a character. First of all, he spoke mostly French, but enough English to get along. He also liked to party late into the night and would typically return to our stateroom after midnight nearly drunk. Usually we were asleep but his bumping around and getting into his bed would awaken us.

A common toilet was located down the corridor about 25 feet so the ship lines placed a porcelain pot in each room in a cabinet with a wash bowl and cold running water. On one occasion Curt spotted George urinating into the sink after his return to the room in a semi inebriated state. We were aghast to think we would wash up in the same sink. When we challenged him with his misbehavior he denied doing it—he probably didn't know what he was doing. But to make a point, the next night when we retired and George was still up on deck dancing, we placed the porcelain pot under his pillow. To our surprise and disbelief, he slept on it all night—it was still there in the morning.

George would kid us that we were going to call "Ulrich." We couldn't figure out what he meant until with motions he explained we would get seasick and regurgitate during the trip. He would constantly ask if we had called Ulrich today. I was fortunate that I did not have that problem for the eight days aboard the vessel. Curt, on the other hand, had to run from the dinner table a couple times to make room for more food.

One night the ship came to a complete stop in the mid north Atlantic and dropped the anchor. The reason for this was due to having spotted small icebergs floating in the region. It was the season of the year (August) when ice from the North Pole would break off and float south. Visibility was poor and this precaution was felt necessary. It only delayed the trip for eight hours, but during that time, many passengers got seasick as the ship just sat and rocked to and fro all night. At daybreak, when visibility improved, we weighed anchor and continued our trip.

The next day was Sunday and we decided to go to the Church of England services being held on board. George asked where we were going and asked if he could go with us, since he had never been to "church" before. What a fiasco!! The service was very formal with a lot of standing, then sitting, then standing and sitting. We tried to follow the program instructions and others in attendance, but George made it difficult. When we would sit, he would remain standing—the only one in the theater. I'd reach over and pull him down. He'd say, "I can't see if I sit." Then it would repeat as we stood and then sat with George still standing. I'd pull him down again. Others were looking at us and wondering who this character was we had with us. Not much worshipping for any of us that morning, including those sitting near us.

The food aboard ship was very good, but sometimes difficult to enjoy. There were invariably persons who were dining and getting seasick. They would rush from the tables and sometimes could not make it to a lavatory or their room before leaving a deposit. The smells began to permeate the dining room and diminish the appetites of those of us who did feel good. We would spend much of our time writing letters and reading. Eight days began to seem a long time.

We finally approached the city of Le Havre, France. We docked there for only a few hours to off-load freight and take on passengers. The ship continued on to the southern port of Southampton in England. From Southampton, we were again able to find and board a train to continue on to London. Our itinerary would have us in England for three or four days before flying south toward West Africa. Upon arrival in London, it was late afternoon and we flagged a cab and gave the address of the hotel in which we were directed to register and stay. The cabbie looked quizzically at the address we gave him and said, "I know the address but I don't know of any hotel in that area." We told him to take us there, which he did and upon arriving at the address we found only an empty lot. It was really a bit depressing.

We were tired from traveling, we were in a foreign country, it was almost dark and we sat looking at an empty lot. Fortunately for us we were in a country, which spoke predominantly English, and had a cabbie that did not try to take advantage of us. I asked the cab driver to deliver us to a hotel, which would be clean and not cost us too much. He did so and we were able to obtain accommodations without any great hassle. We had some difficulty finding a place to bathe and go to the lavatory since the rooms had no such facilities. We walked the corridor from end to end and the only thing we found other than more rooms, were a couple doors marked WC.

We finally learned that WC stood for water closet and the lavatories were in those rooms. Each of them also had a tub for bathing. We found no designation of male or female, so when time came to bathe we just used those facilities and locked the door. One did not spend much time in the WC since all the guests on the floor needed to use the same facility. (We never did find out about the wrong address and hotel and wondered how many other travelers may have been sent there.)

For two days, we battled the fog, drizzle and rain of London to do some sightseeing. We visited all the major attractions in London such as Buckingham Palace, Trafalgar Square, Big Ben, the Tower Bridge, the London Bridge, Westminster Abbey, etc. The only problems we had in London were with the cab drivers. They saw us coming and tried to usurp as much money plus tips as they could get from us. We continually had arguments with them and came to understand they do this all the time with whoever is gullible enough to take their first quote.

Our eagerness to continue our trip was, to a large extent, due to the inclement weather of London and hassles with cabbies. We were eager to board our first major airline for a flight into Africa.

BVS Unit #26, March 1955.

Grace Trimmer and Ivan Fry—our BVS trainers.

Ship "Franconia" sailed from Quebec, Canada, to Southampton, England.

Sara Shisler, missionary from Indian Creek Congregation, 1926-1959.

Ruth Royer Kulp Hospital in Garkida, named for H. Stover Kulp's first wife who died there.

Back of our double house. Left to right, outhouse, watertank, kitchen door.

CHAPTER 5

THE JOURNEY
CONTINUES . . .

The time finally arrived when we were scheduled to leave London. With some difficulty, we engaged a cab to take us to the airport. The driver wanted us to know that to drive us all the way out to the airport would impact on his business in the city. He told us what it would cost, with our heavy luggage, and what his tip would be. He frankly irritated us and we knew we were getting gouged but we knew any other cabbie would similarly try to squeeze us as much as he could, so we agreed. We had a plane to catch! My only comfort was to watch his face as we paid him at the airport when I said, "We were prepared to give you a much more generous tip for helping us with our heavy luggage, but since you were so brazen to *tell us* what your tip would be, here is the tip you requested. Thanks so much." He looked very sad.

The first leg of our flight was aboard a four-engine turbo prop plane flown by British Overseas Airlines (BOAC). For the mid fifties, it was one of the largest passenger planes making intercontinental flights. This flight was my first in a large airliner and I was both a bit apprehensive and eager to experience it. We took off without incident and headed south. Our first stop was scheduled to be Tripoli, Libya, on the shores of the Mediterranean Sea for refueling.

We landed in Tripoli just after the sun had set in the twilight of the day. It was announced that we were allowed to deplane, in that the stop would take about an hour and a half, but we were cautioned not to leave the waiting area inside the terminal. When we exited the plane and walked into the terminal we were met by a soldier armed with an automatic rifle over his shoulder. That was my first experience of seeing such force used at an airport. Today it is quite common. The United States and Britain were at peace with Libya then, but it was a tentative peace. It reinforced that we had best not be walking anywhere other than that lounge.

After freight was exchanged and other passengers boarded, we were off again at about 10 p.m. their time, for Kano, Nigeria. Around midnight, with many of us sleeping, the stewardess came through the cabin, shook our shoulder if we were sleeping and informed us that the captain was having trouble. One engine had already failed and a second was malfunctioning. We were jettisoning all unnecessary fuel, turning 180 degrees and heading back to Tripoli. There would be no smoking allowed due to fuel dump and they hoped they could get back to the airport. At the time we were deep over the Sahara Desert and everyone aboard knew what would be anticipated if we had to crash land in the desert. Nobody was sleeping for the next two hours as we limped back to Tripoli. Needless to say, we made it or I probably wouldn't be writing about it. Back then, and in that location, there was no other plane available to take us on to our destination.

At the expense of the airline, we were all put up in hotels for the day and trips were planned to entertain us until the plane could be repaired. They brought in a huge Rolls Royce engine and proceeded to remove the defective engine and replace it with a good one. In the interim, we were bussed to some ancient ruins for sightseeing, given horse and carriage rides, and some of us even went for a swim in the Mediterranean Sea. The water in the Mediterranean was a bit too warm to be refreshing and was also saltier than the oceans back home. The saltiness adds to the buoyancy when swimming and it is real easy to float on one's back. Well, at least we could say we swam in the Mediterranean Sea and have pictures of Tripoli, Libya. It was, and I suppose still is, a beautiful city, but in recent decades Gadhafi has not been a cooperative ally.

The following morning we again boarded the same aircraft—hopefully properly repaired—and continued our interrupted trip. One benefit was that we could observe the various mountains and valleys, which make up the Sahara Desert as we flew over them. The desert has its own beauty and uniqueness, but is hundreds of square miles of complete desolation. By early afternoon, we flew into the airport at Kano, Nigeria, the northern most International Airport in that country. One more flight still needed to be taken to our next destination. We transferred from the BOAC plane to a much smaller Nigerian Airways plane for the one-hour trip to Jos. When we arrived in Jos, which is the largest city which is closest to the Church of the Brethren Mission Field, I was amazed as I looked out the window of the plane. There was just a sea of wall-to-wall black faces looking up at us from the ground. Among all the natives, two white faces stood out in sharp contrast. I guessed that those two were here to meet Curt and me.

As we disembarked from the plane, a missionary couple that introduced themselves as Charles and Mary Beth Bieber met us. Neither Curt nor I had ever heard of them before then. Mary Beth asked me exactly where it was I called home. I said, "Near Philadelphia in Montgomery County." "No," she said, "where specifically?" I told her it was a small town 25 miles north of Philadelphia called Harleysville. She said, "I taught school in the Harleysville Elementary School for a few years." Small world. I was on the other side of the globe and here was someone who taught in my hometown.

It turns out that I would be working with Charles who was then acting General Secretary at the mission headquarters in Garkida. Curt would be working with Mary Beth as a teacher in the elementary school there while Mary Beth was headmistress. My expectation from prior correspondence and arrangement was that I would be working aside H. Stover Kulp, one of the original missionaries of the denomination to Nigeria. In the interim, however, Stover had moved on to the village of Mubi, where a new campus was being formed and soon would become the center for training native staff and missionaries.

The dirtiest part of our journey faced us before we would get to our new home in Garkida. By jeep, we traveled a couple hundred miles of mostly dirt roads out into "the bush." On these trips you would carry a jerry can of extra gasoline (petrol in Nigeria). There would be no service stations out here and no comfort stations. Restroom stops happened as necessary wherever the brush was thick enough to hide—but watch out for snakes and scorpions. We crossed only a few bridges, all others were concrete swales called drifts. These drifts were usually dry, at least during the dry season, but quickly became flowing streams when rains came. The water flowed across the drifts and you would drive through the water slowly to cross. If the water appeared too deep to safely cross, one of the passengers would get out and slowly walk across the drift to determine the depth, the strength of the flow and if part of the drift had not washed away leaving a crater in its place. If it was questionable, one would place a stone at the water's edge on the drift and could soon determine if the water was receding or getting deeper. There were times in the experiences of each missionary that they waited at such drifts for many hours to safely cross.

It was early in the rainy season when we made the final leg of our trip and the drifts and rivers were not yet a problem. The first Church of the Brethren Mission Station we approached was Waka, the Teacher Training Center at that time. Sara Shisler was a member of the church at Indian Creek in Pennsylvania—also my home church. She had originally arrived on the mission field in the late 20s and worked closely with H. Stover Kulp in the early mission work and translations of the Testaments. Miss Shisler was still teaching natives to become their own teachers and missionaries when I arrived in 1955. I was pleased to bring her greetings from home and she appeared proud to introduce me to others on campus. Most of the translation work was first in the Bura language, the vernacular used in the Garkida area and also at Waka. The language had never been in a written form so the words were spelled phonetically to make it easier for both missionaries and natives to learn, read and speak. Also at Waka were Ivan and Mary Eikenberry and Owen Shankster and his wife and a BVSer by the name of Bob Baker. More about him later.

We waved goodbye for now and continued our journey. We would now descend from the plateau on which Waka is located to the steamier valley areas of Shafa and Garkida. Coming next to Shafa, a small, one family mission station, we met Dick and Ann Burger. The Burgers, with two small children, were a bit isolated but between Garkida and Waka would see more travelers than at some stations. Still almost an hour away and we came into Garkida. Somehow, they knew we were coming and I'll never forget that grand entrance. As we drove along the roadway near Garkida Hospital and into the area near the elementary school, young students from the schools were out along the roadway on both sides, spaced out at arms length, and waving welcomes to us as we arrived. My first impression was that these students all look exactly alike. How will I ever tell them apart? They all had their simple uniforms on with mostly shaved heads. We really felt a special welcome and warmness with this unexpected gesture.

Garkida would be our home for two years. At that time, others on the mission campus there included Herbert and Mari-anne Michael, Charles and Mary Beth Bieber, Charles and Ro-sella Lunkley, Elmer and Ferne Baldwin, Dr. Marvin and Doris Blough and Iris Neff, R.N., as missionaries. The only BVSer on campus when we arrived was Elvis Cayford. Now we were adding Curt Weddle and Ronn Moyer as BVSers. Just one mile away at the Leprosarium Hospital site were Dr. Roy and Violet Pfaltzgraff, Harold (Red) Royer and wife Gladys and V. J. Dick, R.N.

CHAPTER 6

A TOUR OF GARKIDA
AND ENVIRONS

In 1955, Garkida was the largest and central mission station of the Church of the Brethren, about 30 years past the mission's inception. Located in the northeast section of the country of Nigeria, it was not too far distant from the Sahara Desert to the northwest and the country of Chad to the northeast. Being close to the desert area, the soil was sandy and porous for the most part and favorable to most vegetables and tropical trees. It was too hot and humid during the rainy season to grow bananas but most other tropical fruits flourished there. The mission station area was probably about 35 acres with seven family houses for mission staff; an elementary school with grades 1 through 6; a garage or workshop where vehicles were repaired and other equipment serviced; a general hospital with about 30 beds; the headquarters and office building; a very small building used as the post office and another as a guest house for visiting missionaries or other traveling friends.

As we toured the area upon our arrival, we were impressed with the size and scope of the mission station while at the same time surprised at how primitive the facilities were when compared to those of our homes back in the states. For example, there still was no running water or toilet facilities in the missionary houses and electricity was available each night from sunset to ten o'clock (so long as the campus generator worked). The weather was wet from August through January and without a drop of rain the next six months.

During the rainy season, short periods of rain could be expected nearly every afternoon followed by a return of sunshine before the beautiful sunsets. When the rains began, the foliage began turning green and lush and remained that way until the rains ceased around January. The dry season allowed all the vegetation to die and the natives often burned it off. More about that process later. The temperatures varied from morning lows in the 50s in March to highs of 120 Fahrenheit in the shade during August afternoons.

Clothing needs were not a problem. Most of the time, at least during the daytime, the men wore shorts and short sleeve shirts of light colors and the women wore loose fitting summer dresses. Head coverings of some sort were important when outside and footwear was usually sandals or tennis type shoes. When hunting or hiking, high top shoes were better because of both rough terrain and the presence of poisonous snakes. In some cases we were able to obtain fabric and have local natives make shorts for us—so they helped us and we helped them that way.

The central headquarters building was to be my primary workplace. Before you envision an elaborate structure filled with all kinds of office equipment and machines, let me give you a description to help you visualize the scene. The headquarters building was about 16 feet square, divided through the middle by a wall resulting in an office space of about eight by sixteen and a workroom/storage area of similar size. The construction was mud block, which was sun dried and using mud mortar to erect the walls. The walls were then plastered inside and out with a cement coating to protect the mud walls from erosion. A cement floor was poured and a roof of galvanized sheet metal placed on top to form a hip roof.

An entry door with a hasp and padlock and another door was placed in back to receive supplies. Two small desks were in the front for a two-person office and each had a typewriter. In the back workroom was a table on which was a mimeograph machine with a crank handle (remember, no daytime electricity). On the sheet metal roof above was placed a straw mat, woven in sections and tied to the roof to reduce the heat penetration of the sunshine on the roof. There was one window in the office and one in the workroom—basically the only light source—and these windows had no glass panes but only a sturdy screen to keep out pests. I looked at the accommodations of the office I was assigned to, with some angst and question as to how the Lord could use me effectively in this situation.

All of the other homes and structures I mentioned above were similarly built with the interior mud walls and cement coating and pan metal roofing. At one edge of the complex was the old church or meeting place where Sunday Services were held. That building had mud walls without coating and a thick thatch and straw roof. The church was probably about twenty years old and needed replacement. This happened during our two years of service there.

The hospital complex included two wings with beds for patients. Another wing had an operating room including bare bones equipment, but utilitarian enough to handle births, fractures, cuts needing sutures, etc. The scope of treatment and challenge usually went beyond the bounds of the facilities available, but the doctors, without exception, proved to be up to the challenges presented. The disappointing aspect of this care was that even after a presence of years by the mission, many of the incoming patients first tried their various crude home remedies, then went to their witch doctors for help, and finally out of desperation went to the *nasara* "white doctor" for treatment. Too often that methodology brought them to the hospital too late to be of any help and was a frustration to the doctors. An adjunct to the hospital was a small hut, run by trained natives, called a dispensary, to dole out medications and minor treatment during each day of the week. These kinds of dispensaries were also set up at the other mission stations on the mission field.

After touring the campus in the jeep wagon upon arrival, Curt and I arrived at what was to be our home for the next two years. The house was a double house with a large side in which the Biebers lived with their five children and a smaller side in which Curt and I set up housekeeping. We had more room than we needed with a small kitchen area including a small wood stove, an empty dining room with no furniture, a living room with two desks for our use and a small bedroom/bathing area.

Just off the bathing area was an outside verandah area under roof and off the edge of the verandah area an outhouse. There was one single bed in the bathing area, which was to be mine and another on the veranda where Curt would sleep. Each of our beds were equipped with mosquito nets to protect us from mosquitoes. In Nigeria, the bite of the mosquito carries the malaria germ and infection. We would take daily medication to prevent us from getting malaria. It turned out that the medication probably lessened the severity of the disease but at least in my case, did not prevent it.

CHAPTER 7

OUR WELCOME AND STARTING WORK

Upon our arrival we were greeted by a seasonal rain shower, which typically dumped about a quarter inch of rain and quickly subsided into the return of sunshine. A quick get-together was arranged on campus to welcome us to the mission family. A better-planned reception could not happen because those resident in Garkida were not sure if we would arrive when we did, a day later or a week after that. Traveling in August was always a bit uncertain due to rains and local floods. (A bicycler had alerted the primary school children after we had stopped at the Leprosarium on the way to Garkida, just a mile away. They in turn had formed receiving lines along the roadway.) The families of the missionaries met for a picnic to welcome us and to get to know each other. This would be our extended family for the near future.

Greetings to and from our new family of natives happened a couple days later when Sunday morning rolled around and we went to church services in the old church building. We were introduced to the congregation by name and our intended work responsibility. We were not quite sure what was being said about us because the introductions and entire service were conducted in the Bura language. While we could not understand what was being said we could ascertain what was being sung because the tunes were the familiar tunes of the music with which we were familiar. "Jesus Loves Me" and "What a Friend We Have in Jesus" were two that I remember.

We sang along in English and likely nobody noticed because their loud and boisterous singing drowned out any sounds we could make. We were quickly aware that Sunday church services were special to the natives. First of all, many more attended than there was room to seat. Dozens stood outside the open windows and doors singing and praying along with those of us inside. When they sang, it was from the heart and there were no timid singers along with clapping and occasional hand-held drums. From the first hymn we experienced a Spirit-filled worship experience without knowing the language.

The benches in the church were mud brick without backrests. These were not conducive to sleeping during the services. The seats did not conform to the bottom and one could not lean back without hitting the knees of the one sitting directly behind you. About 200 attended that first Sunday we were there. (During the spring of 1994, nearly 40 years later when I visited, there were four times that amount of attendees at Garkida and two new churches had arisen in that interim. At Maiduguri, the largest Church of the Brethren congregation in the world, I experienced a gathering of 2000 plus at the first service, which was followed by another 2000 plus at a second service. Attendance figures were difficult because of the numbers of attendees standing outside around the perimeter of the church building.)

The worship experiences on a Sunday on any of the mission stations were enthusiastic and the event of the week to the natives. They arrived early and in their best clothing. It was almost like an "Easter Parade" every Sunday. Many of the adults and students I learned to know were nearly unfamiliar to me when I saw them at church as opposed to how they dressed during the other six days of the week. They truly praised the Lord!! Their worship services typically included group singing such as the "Women's Ensemble." This involved standing and swaying, clapping small symbols with another on the drums. Congregational singing was always rousing and the ministers bringing the message needed no amplification. It seemed as though qualifications to preach had to include loud penetrating voices, filled with the Spirit and with much arm and body movement to emphasize presentations.

The audience was responsive with their "Amens" and clapping. The colorful wraparound dresses and skirts of the women topped off with colorful bandanas; the mostly white trousers and shirts, topped off by colorful robes for the men; the sandals instead of the usual barefoot; the hand-decorated and sewn skull caps—these all blended into a sea of color offset by the totally black of the skin. No complaint was heard when the worship services lasted an hour and one half or more. The preaching part was usually 40-50 minutes—and loud.

Monday morning following represented my first day on the job in Garkida. An update again; when asked to consider a project in Nigeria, West Africa, before leaving the states, I was told I would be working with Stover Kulp, who along with Albert Helser were cofounders of the mission starting in Garkida in 1924. I was really looking forward to meeting and working with this "Saint of a man" who had given his life to the work in the mission field here.

When I learned, upon arriving in Jos, that was changed and I would now be working with Charles Bieber, I was somewhat disappointed but that changed quickly after having the opportunity to work with "Charlie." Arriving in the office to receive my work assignments from Charlie, it did not take long to show me around the office. As I previously mentioned, it was a small building with space for two office workers and a workroom to do mimeograph and collating work. The mornings were, for the most part, comfortable for shorts and short sleeve shirts. By noon it got really hot and it was typical for us to take a two-hour lunch break during the heat of the day and return for four hours or so mid and late afternoon.

Most days we would get up early and report for prayers with a group of the native workers around 6:30 a.m. We would then grab a quick breakfast and be ready for work around 7:30. Breakfasts were generally a big meal with porridge, cereal or eggs with toast, fresh fruit and coffee. We always had plenty of citrus juice with a citrus orchard on campus and cut up native fruits besides. Our lunch, then, was on the light side with the heat and all and often consisted of guava sauce and homemade biscuits. Again, for supper around 6 or 6:30 we had more to eat. Meat was a precious commodity and scarce. We managed to have good meat two or three times a week. Some of the meat was canned; some was from butchering of beef or chickens when available. Some was from hunting wild game on occasion.

Back to the work assignments: Charles informed me that my first major project would be to print about 75 booklets of the minutes of the annual meetings held on the mission field for the last thirty years since the inception of the mission work in Nigeria. This would take up the bulk of my time for the next couple months at least. Other duties would be to type letters for Charles to the many agencies and churches back in the states, which needed to be contacted on a regular basis. Most of this correspondence was between the offices in Elgin, Illinois, where the Church of the Brethren General Offices were located and the mission headquarters. Most of the funding was channeled through Elgin and it was a constant battle to try to obtain funding for better equipment and salaries for the missionaries and their individual work needs.

The project to produce printed booklets of minutes began with an inventory of supplies. I quickly ascertained we would need about 120 stencils for the Gestetner Mimeograph Machine; a goodly supply of ink for the mimeograph machine and copious amounts of correction fluid if I was to be the one cutting the stencils. I needed to thoroughly clean and keep clean the typeset on the typewriter so the stencils would be cut cleanly. Charles already had laid out the pages so that we could number them as we went and so that we would end up with a table of contents, which accurately showed the correct page numbers. I had to reposition my desk so that I had enough light with which to work since all we had was the illumination from the outside when the shutters were open. If we had to close the shutters for rain or extreme wind we had no light or had to work with the light of the gas lanterns we used each night.

Most of my work was cutting the stencils on the typewriter, which took some time getting accustomed to the feel and capabilities of the machine. This was obviously before electric typewriters or word processing equipment. Charles had the more difficult work of proofing the many years of minutes and getting them into the proper progression of dates and years. Then, we together fitted the rough work into format so that the numbering would work out properly. The layout and prep work itself took some days in the planning before the actual stencil work began.

My recall is that the final booklet had more than 100 pages, so that until we were finished with the table of contents and had separately printed covers on heavier colored paper, we had nearly 10,000 pages to print, collate and bind together. More than 20 reams of paper had to be purchased at the bookstore in

Jos for the job. We would finally use a paper punch and bind the booklet together with twine. At the next Annual Meeting on the mission field, they would be distributed to each missionary family plus the home offices and other arriving mission workers leaving a supply for future needs.

CHAPTER 8

LEARNING THE LANGUAGE —AND OTHER JOBS

D uring the first weeks of orientation, it was planned that we should take some crash course work in learning the local vernacular. The Bura language was confined to a rather small geographical area in the Garkida area and its surroundings. One could hike for a while and be into another language area. In fact, in all of West Africa there are over 200 different language zones. To combat this problem, as people began to become more mobile, these "local" languages were less problematic in that the natives were mostly two or three language people. They, of course, learned their local vernacular and at least one other which was more universal to a larger area. Thus they could travel anywhere in the northern part of Nigeria and if they also knew the Hausa language, they could converse and get along.

When the mission was established, however, in the mid 20s, neither the missionaries nor the natives were very mobile and learning the Bura language alone was quite adequate. Therefore, the books for teaching, the New Testament and the songbooks were written by the early missionaries in the Bura language only. In the mid 50s when we arrived we began to learn Bura since it was used throughout the local area and the primary school children were all using it as their first language in the schools. It would be necessary for those of us in BVS to learn at least enough to be able to teach and converse with the natives. Time was scheduled each week for us to get into classroom mode and study, learn and speak this new language. Marianne Michael, one of the missionaries on campus was good enough to agree to teach us.

During my formative years in Pennsylvania, I was exposed to many people who still spoke in the "Pennsylvania Dutch" dialect—a close relative to the High German, which our forefathers spoke in the "old country" of Germany. I therefore learned some of the Dutch just by being exposed to it over the years. I mention this because in my case at least, almost every time I tried to learn another language, the Dutch word would pop into my mind, if I knew it. As a result, when I wanted to speak a sentence in Bura, I would often insert one or more Dutch words instead. This caused me much frustration for a while but soon I began to know the greetings and common terms.

The schoolboys with whom I worked closely were also helpful. They sensed my struggle and since most of them knew English well enough to converse they gladly suggested the proper translations in Bura. In time that would be helpful since I was asked to consider teaching the fifth grade boys English a few months later.

As time began to pass and we were settling into a routine it was interesting to make new friends with the natives. Even though Curt and I would be primarily working with the schoolboys, we also worked closely with some of the adults and got to know them as close friends. These people sensed and knew from being exposed to the mission work over the past thirty years that we were there to help them and not to take advantage of them. A trust was already in place and the onus was on us young fellows to maintain and build that trust in the time we were there.

We soon learned that there would be many tasks in which we could be helpful. Since I was the "office person" among the newbies on campus, I was asked to assist Maji Kida who was the native charged with receiving the mail each week when the *lorry* arrived. (*Lorry* means "truck" in Oxford English.) Sometimes the truck carrying the mail would arrive and sometimes it would not. All of us on campus, both missionaries and natives, were anxious to receive a letter or package. When the bag or bags of mail did arrive, Maji and I would open the padlocked, one-room building known as the post office and sort the mail into piles for each missionary and the many natives who at that time were receiving weekly mail.

The "post office" was a separate building about four times the size of an outhouse with one table inside. One day in the middle of the dry season, I was sorting the mail with Maji when I noticed that a dark cloud was approaching from the west. I said to him, "Maji, I think we are going to get some rain in a few minutes." I remember him laughing and saying to me, "Mallam Moyer, you have not been here very long and you must understand that it does not rain in the middle of the dry season." About ten minutes later there was about a three-minute downpour of rain. Maji stood in the doorway and as the Nigerians often do when amazed said, "Umm Umm Umm, never have I seen this before!!" I said, "See, I told you" just to rub it in a bit. We both laughed about this unusual phenomenon.

After about two months working in the office, principally on the Annual Conference Minutes project, it became apparent that we would soon complete the booklets desired and that the "other office duties" I was expected to perform, would not take me more than half time, under normal circumstances. It became clear that we needed to find more jobs for me to do to earn my keep.

When speaking of "earning my keep," I am reminded that I should share a bit about the payment system for BVSers in the states and abroad. Again, I relate the norms back in the mid 50s, which are different today. At that time, the BVSers on project in the states received just $15.00 per month for expenses like stamps, toiletries, entertainment, etc. It really did not go very far but the rule of thumb was that BVS is basically an unpaid, volunteer experience. Money from home had to cover clothing and other necessities. The room and board on projects was paid by the project on which the BVSer worked.

I learned, however, that once I got onto the mission field in Nigeria, I would be paid on the basis of a single missionary. That meant that we would receive about $100 per month from the mission board. The difference however, was that we would now need to pay our board, our laundry and ironing and some other routine expenses normally covered for the BVSer on project. The missionary home in which we took our meals would assess us a monthly amount for the meals we ate and we would pay a native boy to do our laundry and ironing. We also paid a "house boy" a stipend each week to come each day and heat our bath water on the wood stove and sweep our house each week. We were able to save a few dollars during the two years but not much.

Primary School in Garkida where I taught 5th grade English.

The Headquarters Building, Garkida.

Sun dried fish at market—for sale. "I can still smell them!"

Baby harnessed antelope

Our next door pet baboon, Pansy.

Pansy, our pet baboon and me.

Bob Baker, Ronn Moyer, Earl Dibert, and Elvis Cayford.

Curt Weddle and Bob Baker at the border of the French Cameroons with Nigeria.

CHAPTER 9

ORCHARD MANAGER AND SCHOOLTEACHER . . .

A s mentioned, the Administrative Assistant responsibilities in the general office at Garkida were soon compacted into a half time position. In looking for additional responsibilities for me to undertake, it was suggested that I consider managing the citrus orchard. Never having worked with Torrid Zone fruit trees but always being interested in trees, shrubs and vegetable gardens I was intrigued with the challenge and accepted the responsibility readily. The orchard was a tract of the mission area fronting on the Hawal River and was about two to three acres in area. It was in the flood zone and therefore remote from the main mission area by about 400 yards. The hospital, church and missionary houses were east of the orchard on a gentle slope not threatened by the river overflow.

A cactus fence enclosed the orchard, which was a deterrent to the hogs and goats. They ran unleashed throughout the neighborhood. When certain fruits were bearing and falling to the ground, these animals had a way of getting through the cactus and filling their stomachs on the mission's fruit supply. One of my jobs was to try to better secure the perimeter "fencing" and keep the fruit supply secure. This was very difficult since I could not be patrolling the boundary continually.

On one occasion I shot a pig with my .22 rifle. This pig was often getting into the orchard and I was trying to discourage it and others from coming in. It turned out that the shot killed the animal, which belonged to one of the men in the village nearby. While this may not have been a good thing to do from the perspective of being a good neighbor, it did have the impact of causing some of the families in the village to fence in their animals, which is what they should have been doing. I took the position with the natives that allowing their animals to roam freely and eat other person's foodstuffs and fruit was really no different then stealing.

The work needing to be done within the orchard included carrying water to water the trees and plantings during the dry season, trimming and pruning the trees as needed, picking the various fruits as they became ready to eat and carrying the fruit up to the main campus to be distributed. This work required me to hire men each week to get the job done. Each Monday morning, after prayers, the native men who wanted to work for wage, gathered at the workshop.

I had a "head man" who worked for me in the orchard every day, every week as a full time permanent worker. He would consult with me each Monday morning about the work needing to be done and how many men would be needed to get it done. The head man would then select from those gathered desiring to work the number of men he would need for that day or that week. Usually he would select two to six depending on the season— whether more fruit was coming in and whether a lot of water needed to be carried. The men used five-gallon tins with a handle on the top and carried the tins on their heads from the river adjacent to the orchard to the trees needing water.

The various types of trees and fruits included the entire citrus line of grapefruits, oranges, limes, tangerines and lemons.

Other trees included mangoes, guava and papaya. The tree-ripened mango is similar in taste to the peach but more fibrous. The papaya is similar in taste to the muskmelon. Each day—Monday through Friday—these fruits were picked off the ground and picked off the trees and brought by the workers to the main part of the campus for distribution. They were put into large bushel-size baskets, placed on the men's heads and brought to one of the missionary's houses where they carefully emptied them on the verandah. It was my job to sort out the fruits as equitably as I could and then have them delivered to the various missionaries' houses at the station. Some weeks there was little to distribute due to the changing of the seasons, but most of the days there was a nice supply for each family.

Another part of my job was to supervise the workers, unannounced from time to time to be sure they were doing their work. On occasion I would find them sitting under a tree, but the head man was responsible to keep them occupied and he did a good job.

I learned that the papaya could be planted from seed and grown to supply fruit in about one year. We all recognized that the average native to whom we were preaching and teaching had a meager diet and mostly starches. In an effort to promote better nutrition among the villagers, I suggested to Curt that we plant a number of papaya seedlings and then plant them in the compounds of the natives ourselves so they could have some fresh fruit within the next year. I planted the seeds in the orchard near the river and was amazed to experience an almost 100% germination.

When the seedlings were about twelve inches high, we transplanted between 200 and 300 into the compounds of all those who would allow it and most of them seemed very grateful. We insisted they must protect the seedlings from the roaming animals. Most of them took immediate steps to protect them. Sadly, however, when we checked on their growth success a few months later, most of them had been nibbled off and destroyed. It was a disappointing realization that fruit in their diet was just not important to them. Well, at least some of them survived and did bear some fruit so it was not a total waste.

Once the orchard work was running smoothly and we had some semblance of responsible workers knowing they would be supervised, I again had spare time and began looking for work. About that time one of the missionaries went on furlough and there was a shortage of teachers for the elementary school. The Biebers and Lunkleys challenged me to accept the role of teaching fifth grade English to take up the slack. I applied to the governing agency for Northern Nigeria for a teaching certificate. I was able to get copies of my transcripts and grades from high school in the States and from the various colleges at which I had received college level credits.

It was not long until I received a teaching certificate and began preparing for part time teaching. The school system was regulated by the governing authorities, which at that time were British—Nigeria being a British subject. (Their independence was just a couple years away.) This meant that the teaching would need to be according to the Oxford English methods and alphabet and not the American English system. Instead of "schedules" we had "sheddules;" and you say "neether" and we say "nither" but spell it neither and instead of "x y z" we say "x y zed." There were other differences but it did not present major problems.

The first day in the classroom, I went from being a *mdirki* to being a *mallam*. That is, from a "man of the house" to a "teacher." Just like that I was Mallam Moyer. I didn't feel much like a teacher and probably was more anxious than the little guys in the front row whose big white eyes stood out against the black skin.

Those days, it was mostly all boys—at least in my class—and the ages of the class ranged from 11 to 20. I had about 20 boys and it was customary for the smaller, younger boys to sit in front and the larger, older boys sat to the back. The reason for the range in age happened because sometimes these boys were 14 or 15 years old before they started school since there were no mandatory education criteria as in the states.

My responsibility was primarily to help these young fellows get to a point where they could speak English understandably and be able to understand others who were speaking it. I tried to make the class more interesting by interjecting new words which required having interesting discussion such as snow; ocean; mountain; jet airplane; skiing; baseball; golfing; volcano or any word that represented something with which they were totally unfamiliar. Some of these students had never traveled more than a few miles in their entire lifetimes. I remember one day one of the younger 11 year olds raised his hand and asked the question, "Mallam Moyer, what is the meaning of the word 'the'?" How do you go about explaining that question?

The most difficult parts of learning English for these boys were words that were pronounced the same and spelled differently such as for—four—fore or two—to—too or read—red. Words that were spelled the same but pronounced differently such as read and read. The other difficulty was the use of idioms such as "hit the sack" or "straight from the horse's mouth" or "the last straw" and literally thousands of others we use every day without thinking about how difficult this might be for someone learning the language. Of course, it was necessary for me to know most of the common words of the Bura language to be able to interpret for them. I therefore, had to do more studying on my own to learn what they were saying and asking. By the fifth grade, however, the boys had already learned enough English that we could help each other. Sometimes they helped me with a word and sometimes I could help them.

Working with boys individually as time went by, I became rather close to them. At the time I was only 21 years old myself. Many of these boys came from a distance and lived in the boys' quarters (a barracks like building), which just happened to be located very close to our house. This allowed the boys to wander over to our place in the evenings and sometimes I would walk over to their quarters and we would just sit around and "shoot the bull" or "chew the fat"—a couple more idioms. This was also opportunity to share our faith and reasons why we had come to help them instead of going into the military. Many deep and meaningful questions were asked and discussed in those "skull sessions." After leaving the mission field, we had the satisfaction of knowing we had the opportunity to be a witness and example to the young fellows and help them to get a good start in their lives. Many of them became preachers and deacons in their churches and also went into professions such as law and medicine.

CHAPTER 10

MARKET DAY . . .

The natives at Garkida were fortunate when it came to shopping. Once a week, the market came to town as many lorries (trucks), a few camels, many bicycles and many more on foot arrived soon after dawn and set up in a large field especially used for this purpose. In our culture in the states today we would call this a large flea market. Many of the more sophisticated vendors brought poles and tarpaulins or straw mats for shelter from the sun for the long day ahead. This group of vendors would move each day to another location and set up all over again. Tuesday was the day for Garkida. On a few occasions I went to the market place and took pictures (reference photo section).

It was a unique experience to visit the marketplace and to observe the myriad selections of almost anything the natives might need. One of the most forgettable displays to me was that of the butcher. It was typical to see the various parts of a goat or a cow displayed on the ground with flies covering each part to the point of nausea. A cow's head might be lying there with the eyes looking at you and the tongue hanging out. A hunk of meat from the leg might be lying next to that so covered with flies you could hardly see the meat.

Next booth might be a seller of fabric. Fabrics imported from Europe through Lagos, the capital city at the time, were offered, as well as native woven cotton fabrics; some of which had been dyed indigo. This booth usually included a foot treadle sewing machine with a merchant willing to do some sewing for you as needed.

Other booths included implements forged by local blacksmiths such as blades for hoes, knives and axes. The native hoe was a round steel blade about 5 inches in diameter with a short handle of 30 inches. To plant their guinea corn (sorghum) one needed to bend over, slap the hoe into the ground with the right hand, throw in a few seeds with the left, cover it again with the hoe in the right hand and move on, all in one fluid series of motion, until the entire patch or field was planted. This chore was the responsibility of the wives and often with a small baby tied to their backs as they planted.

Another booth in the marketplace would display native made jewelry such as beads for necklaces and bracelets. Cheap imports were sometimes available such as watches and rings. The women liked to dress up when they could, with bracelets up their arms and anklets, necklaces and earrings galore. Top that off with a flashy imported and colorful bandanna, a flowered *zhebi* (wrap around cloth garment) and "walla," we're ready for church.

All kinds of foodstuffs from hot peppers to guinea corn were displayed and usually a lot of bananas. Seldom, however, could you find the delicious and appetizing fruits and vegetables to which we were accustomed. Many days I would have given a couple dollars for a good apple. Sorry, not available. Many of the missionaries tried planting their own gardens with sweet corn, string beans, peas, lettuce and the like. It usually was an exercise in futility however. The natives were wont to allow their pigs and goats to roam freely through the compounds and mission areas so that the gardens became food for the animals before they matured for the missionaries' use.

One of the most popular booths or areas of the market area was the homemade beer. On the morning of the market, as many local vendors were walking down the dirt road toward the market area, you could see women with huge half-gourds slowly walking to the market balancing the large pots on their heads. One day I was driving the jeep from Garkida to the Leprosarium on a Tuesday, when I happened to come up behind two of these ladies carrying their beer to market. At a short distance, I tooted the horn since they were walking down the middle of the road. They were talking to each other and laughing and paid me no attention. As I got closer, still no response. Now I was within 10 feet of their backs, driving the same speed as they walked, afraid to blow the horn a third time as it might startle them. Soon, other market goers yelled at them to move.

One slowly turned so as not to drop the gourd of beer, saw the front of the jeep and started yelling and at a slow trot weaved from one side of the road to the other finally choosing the market side to get off the roadway. During this time, I really felt sorry for her since she was spilling a copious amount of beer down over her head. She never dropped the gourd, however, and saved most of it for her day's income. She stood there with her hand over her heart laughing her eyes out. I yelled, *"Bwashang mwala,"* ("sorry lady") and slowly drove on. The natives nearby thought this was the funniest thing they had seen in a long time and were roaring with laughter at the expense of the beer-soaked woman vendor. Well, perhaps that shortage of brew saved someone from getting drunk that day, who knows.

Other vendors included pottery—large displays of fire hardened pots of all sizes were displayed; mechanics to repair bicycles with parts and wrenches needed; footwear of all kinds from sandals to imported, cheap shoes, leather items from belts to pelts for sale—the leather mostly used was goat skins which were tanned and very pliable for use in a variety of ways. These vendors displayed leather items such as wallets and purses, some of which were quite nice really and purchased often as souvenirs by tourists.

One of the unforgettable booths or displays was the fish market. Most of these fish were netted in Lake Chad, north of Nigeria, and hauled to market by camel. The process was to catch the fish, lay them on the sand under the 130 degree sun and allow them to dry completely to a crisp. They would then bag them, put them on the camels and bring them many miles to market. One can only imagine the aroma. How anyone could eat the fish was beyond me. Some natives would make a dip from the fish to eat with their porridge.

Most of all, market day was a celebration of fun and food. Nearly everyone in the villages surrounding the Garkida area showed up to sit around and talk and tell stories. In retrospect, I find it similar to going "to the mall" in contemporary society. Late in the afternoon, the vendors would pack up their wares preparatory to moving to the next village for the Wednesday market. The local vendors would not follow, as the distance was too great—in some instances 20 to 30 miles distant. The itinerate merchants who had trucks or camels and made it their business would be traveling throughout the week.

CHAPTER 11

BEWARE OF THE SNAKES!

Living full time in northern Nigeria, it is important to understand the dangers of this foreign country and be cautious. Dangers range from the medical/physical through awareness of wild animals to people with different beliefs without moral compass.

One of the most obvious and feared dangers is that of snakes. Basically, there are three different groups of snakes slithering throughout the area. One is the family of python snakes, which grow to be extremely large but are not poisonous. The elephant python, which is in the area, often grows to a length of fifteen feet or more and they are known to swallow small animals whole allowing their digestive system to break down the tissue of its victim. The python also will defend itself by wrapping itself around its victim and causing suffocation by squeezing tightly. In the immediate area in which our mission was located it was rare to ever see these pythons, however, I was able to obtain a few skins which were tanned and good for making belts, purses, wallets, shoes and other leather items. These were about 12 feet long and 15 inches wide. This obviously would mean that the living python has a body up to 6 inches in diameter—a rather scary thought.

The second variety would be the cobra family and the third the vipers. Both of these have bites, which can be deadly within hours or minutes depending on where bitten and if any anecdote is available immediately. The "spitting cobra" is also dangerous from a distance of up to 10 feet because if cornered, it wants to spit its venom at the person or animal that is threatening them. This cobra spits the venom at the eyes of the victim in an effort to blind the aggressor so that it can get away or protect its young. When a human gets this venom in the eyes, it is not usually fatal, but will cause blindness and pain over an extended period of time—again depending on how soon it is treated.

One evening soon after it had become dark; about the time Curt and I were preparing to go to bed, we had a visitor, which was not welcome. As previously shared, his "bedroom" was on the outside verandah, which was under roof and mine was just inside the door in the bathing area of our house. Curt called to me and with some trepidation stated, "Come out here a minute, it sounds as though someone is in the privy." I came out onto the verandah and we stood there for a minute and listened. Then we heard a noise, which sounded like someone breathing very hard as if they had just run a long distance and were winded. Indeed the noise seemed to come from the outhouse, which was attached to the end of the verandah.

The outhouse was built so as not to need to use doors. Ours was a one-seat toilet with walls like a short maze. You entered then turned left and left again to sit down. This way you had privacy without the need of a door. Wood for doors was difficult to come by and expensive. Under the seat was a bucket, which was emptied every day by a workman who limed the bucket and the enclosure to keep it clean as possible. On the outside was a hinged door to enclose the bucket from animals or children. It was quite a good arrangement. I digress in this manner so that you can try to follow the next sequence in our adventure of "Who's in our privy?"

I reached inside our back door and got a club we had there for wild animals or intruders. I also got my flashlight and with the club in my right hand and the flashlight in my left, I began to call out to whoever was inside to come out. I got no response so I started to enter shining the flash around the corner with the club raised. Nobody was inside. I paused a moment and again heard the heavy breathing sound, now coming from beneath the toilet seat. I slowly lifted the seat shining the light toward the bucket underneath. There was nothing in the bucket, but I saw movement aside the bucket and quickly realized that a spitting cobra was coiled around the bucket on the floor. The next hissing sound was the spitting of the venom, but it was directed at the flashlight since the snake could not see my eyes, blinded by the light. I slammed the seat cover and quickly backed out of the outhouse exclaiming to Curt that a spitting cobra was under the seat. What to do now!!!

We had no idea how it got there or how long it would stay there, but recognized the danger to ourselves. I suggested that we try to shoot it with the .22 rifle we had for short hunting trips and small game. I loaded the rifle as we went back outside and the plan was that Curt would knock open the trap door on the outside after I was set with the rifle. I held the rifle ready with my flashlight alongside the barrel ready for action. Curt ran by and kicked open the door wherein the bucket sets. I carefully aimed alongside the bucket, not wanting to put a hole in our waste receptacle, and fired a shot.

The shot grazed the body of the cobra causing it pain and it began to slither out the door towards me. It was spitting its venom so I stayed back about 15 feet. As it slowly slithered out and hit the ground, I shot three more shots. The cobra rolled over and lay still. I thought it might be playing possum and was cautious for a minute or two. We approached finally and found it was dead. One bullet went through the head and the other right behind the head. I looked skyward and breathed a thank you prayer to the Lord. I knew and realized that I am not that good a shot in the dark with a wiggling target. The Lord was protecting us and He was an excellent marksman.

You can believe that from that night on, we carefully entered our outhouse and *always* checked under the seat before we sat down in there. About two weeks after that episode, one evening at dusk as I was visiting the outhouse, I carefully scanned the approach to the outhouse and saw a movement. Indeed, it was a tiny cobra about eight inches long. It quickly disappeared in a crack. The little ones can be just as deadly as the large ones. Fortunately, we had no more of that excitement.

During our term in Garkida, some of us shared a desire to build a permanent tennis court for recreation when we had time. There had been such a court cleared nearby but it was not paved and the wet/dry seasons had not been kind to it. There were about ten of us on the mission station who had varying degrees of interest, so we pooled our funds and ordered the cement necessary to build a cement slab court. Cement was very expensive at that time due to the fact it had to be imported. As we were clearing the area of rocks and debris preparing to lay the foundation, some of us were picking up stones and throwing them into the wheelbarrow, when Dr. Blough arrived to help us. He was also a tennis player and part of the tennis gang.

Dr. Blough saw what we were doing and yelled for us to stop. "Why?" someone said. He said, "Don't pick up those rocks like that and throw them into the wheelbarrow. You need to turn over the rocks first with a shovel or rake to be sure no snakes are hiding underneath." A couple of us looked at each other and rolled our eyes, thinking, I guess we will have to follow his advice—at least as long as he is here—to humor his suggestion. Would you believe, no more than half a dozen rocks were turned over when one of the helpers jumped back because underneath that rock was a small viper hiding and ready to spring. It was an "I told you so" moment for Doc. It was another "Hand of God" protection to all of us. There most likely would have been a tragedy had not Doc showed up and cautioned us. The viper was killed with a shovel but was the type whose bite could have been fatal within an hour.

One day one of the native men working with a group of men building a small building on campus lifted a wooden rafter from the ground and was bitten by such a viper. He immediately walked away toward his home telling others he would be OK but needed to get some "medicine" for the bite. He returned the next day to work again and surprised all the others because he seemed none the worse from the incident. When quizzed about what he did or where he went to get treated, he only shared that he got the roots of a couple plants he used to make a mixture and drink it. He said he got sick during the night but the medicine made him better so now he can work. He would not share what the mixture was as it was a family secret handed down through generations. Dr. Blough was upset that he could not obtain the information and perhaps help others with the same problem, but the man remained adamant that he could not share.

Everyone who has lived in Nigeria for any period of time has his or her own snake stories. A new missionary couple came to the field for the first time during my stay there. We had a special time of invitation, dinner and celebration for their safe arrival and wishes for a good term in the field. After eating a sumptuous meal, the women seemed to congregate around the kitchen and the men sat on the front porch at the Lunkley residence, which was close to our house. We got to talking about our various snake stories which Bob, the new missionary found interesting.

About a month later, when Bob and his wife again visited the Garkida station, Bob's wife told us about a nightmare Bob had that first night after our sharing snake episodes. She said during the night, Bob suddenly sat straight up in bed, grabbed the wrist of his left arm with his right hand in a strangle hold and began shaking his left wrist saying, "I got him, I got him," as he completed a dream about a snake getting after him. Bob had to laugh but also admit that it happened and was somewhat embarrassed about it. We all got a good laugh at his expense.

CHAPTER 12

OTHER WILDLIFE . . .

Having always been an avid outdoorsman and hunter, I was eager to do some hunting in the areas surrounding our mission station. Not long after I began teaching in the primary school, the students alerted me to opportunities for small game within walking distance of our house. A few weeks after the rains had begun in the rainy season, the new grasses were about 12 to 15 inches tall and afforded good hiding cover for the wild guinea fowl and quail.

I engaged one of the older students as a guide to show me where such game might be found and he eagerly agreed, partly because it might mean fresh meat for him. I was able to borrow a .16 gauge shotgun from one of the missionaries and we were on our way. After a trek of just a couple miles we began to ascend up to a plateau area with grassy sides and only a few trees. The walking was difficult because of the multitudinous rocks of baseball to football size hiding in the grass. As we approached the top I could hear the chattering of the wild guineas and motioned to my guide to squat and wait so I could look over the top before they might see him. I raised the shotgun and slowly and quietly inched myself forward until the plateau above was at my eye level and waited.

Just ahead, within good shotgun range, there appeared the heads of a small flock of guinea fowl popping up to look around and tucking their heads back down to remain invisible. I made a slight sound as I removed the safety and as about six to eight fowl popped up their heads just 25 feet ahead I fired. The result was that I was able to kill two and wound two with only one shot. My guide ran into the confusion and captured the wounded ones so that we had four nice guinea fowl to carry back for future meals.

I gave one to the student guide from which he made a *sukwar* (a gravy-like mix into which the natives would dip their chunky porridge with their fingers and then into the mouth). It also gave him a chance to share fresh meat with the other students. I was able to share the other fowl with the two missionary families who were responsible for feeding us BVSers. It was a worthwhile hunt and a treat since fresh meat was difficult to find on a regular basis.

Other edible game in the immediate area included two or three varieties of gazelle. These ranged from the smallest—about the size of a medium to large size dog—up to the largest, which was similar to the American Whitetail deer in size. One afternoon I was hunting when I spotted a lone gazelle grazing on the opposite hillside. The Thompson's Gazelle was a bit too far away to waste a cartridge of the 30-40 Krag, military type rifle I was using. I slowly began to inch down the slope I was on to get closer but there was little or no cover and upon spotting me the gazelle ran over the top of the slope he was on and down the other side.

I continued to the top only to find him on the opposing slope, still about 300 yards away. I could tell that I would not get closer in this terrain so I set the open peep site on the rifle to its 200-yard capacity, then raised the barrel about an inch and squeezed the trigger. The gazelle instantly fell flat and did not move. I could not believe I could even hit it, much less bring it down. I quietly and slowly sneaked forward until I was just a few feet away and noted that the eyes were open and it was completely alert. I had severed the spine with the shot and paralyzed the gazelle.

I quickly cut the throat to finish the job and was able to carry the animal home on my back. This gazelle was full size, but they only grow to about 50 to 80 pounds and are extremely fleet afoot. The guide with me just put his hand over his mouth and muttered, "Umm Umm Umm." I asked him what was the matter and he said in Bura, "Now I know you are a man!! I did not believe any *bindigu* (gun) could reach that far." I assured him that it was a very lucky shot, that I had surprised myself. However, when we returned to camp he could not get finished telling everyone what a great hunter I was to the point it was embarrassing. Well, again, it provided meat for the table, which was welcome. Canned meats were more typical of our menus when we had meat at all.

Other wild animals existing in the area included hyena, leopard, baboon, monkeys, geese, ducks and an occasional lion. At some distance elephants, giraffe, water buffalo and wild boar could be hunted. Special, very expensive licenses were required to hunt and shoot these larger animals. I was not able to hunt these animals due to time, license, travel and costs. Of course, it would have been fun but I was not in Nigeria to go hunting and I was just happy to be able to do some of the more minor hunting, which I did.

One of the other game birds I enjoyed hunting were the spur-winged geese. These geese were comparable in size with the Canadian geese in North America. The big difference was that they were all white with razor sharp spurs on the first knuckle of the wing. These geese used this spur as a weapon for self-defense and would charge with their beak and their wings flapping. It was interesting to sneak through swamps and try to get a shot at them. Sometimes multiple geese were bagged with one shot if one could get close enough and shoot once, while they were swimming close together, once when they were taking off (when their wings were most vulnerable to breaking) and a last shot as they rose above. The fun began when one was wounded in the wing and unable to fly but quite adept at swimming underwater for long stretches. They would go under and resurface twenty feet away; then do it again until finally captured either with another shot or by hand.

The most dangerous of the animals, other than poisonous snakes, were the baboon. They were dangerous because they traveled in packs and attacked in packs. They were known to attack and kill other animals such as lions or water buffalo because they did it en masse. Individually, the baboon grew to about five feet standing on their hind legs and would weigh about 100 pounds. Charles Lunkley, our neighbor missionary, had captured a small baboon a year or so before we arrived and had it tied to the tree off their verandah. They named it Pansy, and she was an enjoyable pet during our stay in Garkida.

Pansy was about 2 feet tall and 20 pounds during that time and it was amazing how much like a human she was. Charles had affixed a wooden box on one of the lower limbs to give protection from the rain and sun and in which Pansy could sleep. We would hold Pansy or let her sit on our shoulder (when she would automatically begin sorting through the hair on our head searching for fleas as they are wont to do). She also was a bit mischievous when she had the opportunity.

One day I observed Pansy hiding behind her tree and saw that an old blind native woman was coming up the path with her long stick probing in front of her. I just stepped back and watched. As the blind beggar woman approached the Lunkley house, looking for a handout, Pansy patiently waited until she was within the range of her chain. Pansy then quietly walked in front of her, grabbed the walking stick and tugged on it two or three times, then let it go. The blind woman said in her native tongue, "Who is that? Who is pulling on my stick?" Pansy just looked up at her and grunted in her throat, which she often did when excited or happy.

Then Pansy did it again and this time the lady began to swing the stick and Pansy ran behind the rock next to the tree and, so help me, she had a smile on her face showing her teeth and grunted again. Finally, as I was about to step in and tell the woman what was happening, Pansy raced out from behind her rock, grabbed the blind woman's *zhebi* (the cloth they wrap around themselves and tuck in at the shoulder) gave a good yank and the whole *zhebi* came off, leaving the blind woman naked except for a g-string. Pansy ran up the tree with the *zhebi* and sat on her branch literally laughing at the poor woman. The blind woman was shaking her stick and talking very fast and loud to whoever was tormenting her. I stepped in, took hold of Pansy's chain and scolded her. She let go of the *zhebi* and I handed it back to the woman trying to explain that a pet baboon had done this and not a human. Between my faulty language ability and trying to make her believe a baboon had done this, well, I think she still thinks I did it.

During our stay, another missionary, John Grimley, was returning from Uba to Lassa on his motorcycle. On that bush road there is one spot where an earthen formation next to the road is an obvious oddity. The total area is flat as a pancake, but at this one spot there is a large mound of ground slowly rising from grade to about 25 feet high with a sharp drop off in front. It appears as though a large earthmover was there years ago and left a deposit. Anyway, it was a nice day and John had his camera along so he stopped his cycle near the road at the blunt end of the mound, walked around to the rear and climbed up the grade to the top to see what picture opportunities might be there.

He was not there but a few minutes when he heard the grunt of multiple baboons. He looked behind him in the direction he had just come up the grade and saw that a pack of baboons was coming to have him for lunch. There was only one way to move and he needed to move quickly. That was down the drop off on the road side. He slid and bounced on his butt all the way to the bottom, ran to his motorcycle, jumped on, kicked the starter lever and was extremely surprised that it started on the first kick, which almost never happened. He put it in gear and raced away as fast as he could. He looked behind him to see that the closest baboon was only a few feet behind, but losing pace quickly. John said it was the hand of God that started the cycle on the first kick or he would have been in big trouble.

The crocodile experience episode comes later— don't miss it.

Jaffa Falls, natural wonder, where we swam with the crocodiles.

Swimming below Jaffa Falls (with the crocodiles).

1956 Annual Conference at Garkida

Seven BVSers gathered at the Annual Conference from the entire mission area.

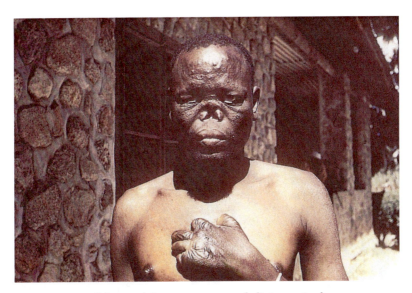

Advanced Leprosy, nose and digits typical.

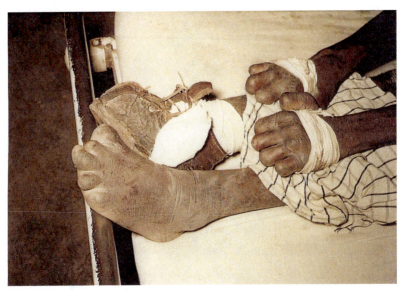

Leprosy patient—note the left hand's large finger has two joints missing but fingernail exists.

Dr. Marvin Blough next to a 10-foot ant hill.

CHAPTER 13

GODS—CHRISTIAN/PAGAN

During the 1950s, some 30 years after the Church of the Brethren Mission began in northern Nigeria, the local natives still had strong beliefs in "other gods." Most of these natives in the mission area were professing Christians, having been baptized over the years on their profession of faith in Christ. Only generations later did this belief or fear in pagan gods begin to finally disappear. One evening after dinner, I sat with some of the older schoolboys and discussed this subject. The boys in the school compound were about 12 to 15 years of age and at least 10 of them gathered around.

These students came from various different geographical areas (all within 50 miles), but that was distant enough to exhibit different stories about gods. These stories had been told from generation to generation in the different families.

One god was a god of protection and was used to help prevent theft. I don't remember the names of these gods, but this one was to be feared as powerful enough to cause death or catastrophe to a thief or robber if caught. If you had a possession which might easily be stolen such as a bicycle or new shoes or money; when you were unable to attend to them, you could protect them as follows: You would select three stones—large, medium and small and place them atop one another to form a pyramid with the large stone on the bottom, topped by the medium stone and the small stone or pebble on top. You would place this pyramid of stones on the object you wished not to be stolen. You would then call upon this god to bring a curse or death on any potential robber and leave your possession with assurance that it would not be stolen. It was amazing that this almost always worked and theft was not a big problem.

Another god was one who would appear only with the moon phase. The god would be in a certain tree near the marketplace area after dark. It was a night when nobody would go near the marketplace—indeed, the boys I talked with said they normally went indoors after nightfall and stayed there for fear of this god. I asked what the god looked like and they did not know but indicated a ghost through which you could see. The boys said to go near this god would be certain death and the god was there to see in the dark and determine who was bad so as to bring sickness and death to them.

I was interested in this story and asked the boys if they would go with me if I went to this place to observe this god. One young fellow of 15 said, "No, no, Mdirki, you will surely die if you go." I suggested that I would take a gun along if they would go with me and show me the place. Finally two of the boys said they would, even though I saw fear in their eyes. When the time came for its appearance, the two boys were nowhere to be found so I never did get to see what they were afraid of, since without their assistance I didn't know where this tree was located. I didn't pursue it further, because I knew it would be a waste of time in any event. I was just trying to rid them of this fear and of this old tale.

The one god about whom they shared stories did intrigue me. It was an unnamed god. This god had been close and helpful but now was distant and angry. I was reminded of the story of Paul in Acts 17, as he stood on Mars Hill in Athens and said, "Men of Athens! I see that in every way you are very religious. For as I walked around and looked carefully at your objects of worship, I even found an altar with this inscription: TO AN UN-KNOWN GOD. Now what you worship as something unknown I am going to proclaim to you."

The boy's story to me went something like this: Many years ago there was a god who was very close to us. This god protected us from the hyena and the baboons and caused our crops to grow. He kept illness at bay and maintained peace with the neighboring tribes. We were responsible to feed this god, so each night we set out at a certain place, a bowl of *diva* (a thick porridge made from guinea corn or sorghum). Each morning the bowl was empty, so we knew that this god was being fed. (Of course nobody ever saw anyone or anything eat from the bowl since it was at a secret place where nobody could go except the person delivering the food.)

Their *diva* was a staple and the natives also ate this twice a day unless they happened to have a special occasion with fresh killed meat of some sort. Usually, the men would sit in a circle with a large bowl of this porridge in the middle. They would reach into the bowl with their fingers, break off a piece about the size of a golf ball, dip it into the *sukwar* in a separate bowl and pop it into their mouths. The *sukwar* was a gravy-like mixture of whatever was available like meat pieces, herbs, water, vegetables, etc. In this way they usually did not use any utensils. Anyway, back to this god who was close, then distant.

One day the person responsible to place the food out for the god was too lazy to wash the bowl and bits of porridge had crusted in the bowl. When the god thrust his fingers into the *diva*, his fingernails and fingers were cut due to the crusty bowl and they began to bleed. This so angered the god that he left their area and went far away and now they could not readily access him any longer. The person who was responsible to set out the food, found the bowl with blood marks on it and on the stone upon which it was setting.

Since then, there has been more sickness, wild animal assaults and crop failures than before. They wish this god would return to them and be close again. Does the story of disappointing god, being far from Him, then repenting and having Him forgive us and being close to us again, sound like a good application for mission work? We were able to tell them the name of their god and how to get close again. Praise the Lord!!

It is interesting that almost all pagan peoples the world over have stories about one or scores of gods. These stories are passed down by word of mouth to succeeding generations. In many cases it is only a messenger or missionary who is needed to interpret their stories and tell of the one true God. When that happens—if it is done unselfishly and prayerfully—these peoples are awakened to our Savior and are eager to learn the work of God. The ingredient needed is that person to go and teach them.

CHAPTER 14

BITS AND PIECES

Many stories come to mind, which happened over a two-year period of time (fall of '55 to fall of '57) but, while interesting and noteworthy, are not related and not worthy of a whole chapter.

Regarding personal health and potential for trouble, I am reminded of concerns endemic to this equatorial region. For one, the threat of contracting malaria was not a happy thought. Not everyone who lives in these torrid areas for long periods of time experiences malaria but most do to some degree. By way of explanation of that comment, let me explain. Prior to traveling to Nigeria, I was required to have about five different shots or inoculations. Such concerns as yellow fever, malaria, river sickness and other tropical diseases/ailments are a threat. Prior to arrival in Nigeria, I was started on daily medication to prevent malaria. After arrival and every day during our stay the medication continued and finally continued for about a month after returning to the states upon completion of the project term.

This medication, as explained to us, would not necessarily prevent us from contracting malaria but would lessen the effects if we did get it. During my two years, I contracted malaria twice. If the medication I was taking softened its effects, I dread to consider what it would have been like without the malaria medications. One day, when the outside temperature was around 120 degrees Fahrenheit, I started a fever, which topped 104 degrees. Dr. Blough informed me that I had malaria—to be quiet, to rest and to drink plenty of fluids.

I began to get cold and shiver. I lay in my bed and piled on the blankets although the bedroom temperature was near 100. I shivered and shook for about a half hour, then got extremely hot, threw off the covers and nearly all my clothes and perspired profusely. No air conditioning—indeed no electricity for a fan during the daytime. After another half hour of sweating, I again got cold, got back into bed, piled on the covers and shivered for 30 minutes or so. This sequence of hot and cold continued for two to three days until it began to level off.

Since I could not eat much during this experience, I finally returned to normal about a week later, but having lost 10 pounds and was very weak. The second time I got malaria fever, it was not as severe, thankfully, and didn't last as long, but I was able to empathize with others and families of the natives who had children die from malaria. Every night we slept under mosquito netting to prevent bites from the mosquitos carrying the malaria germs.

Wet Season/Dry Season: As I already mentioned, a one-year cycle in northern Nigeria included about six months of rainy days and six months without rain. Usually the dry season never had a drop of rainfall the entire six-month period. After the rains stopped and the dry season started, around the Christmas season or middle January, all the vegetation, which was not watered or irrigated, died off to straw colored weeds and dead plants. The natives would often burn the dead grasses, using field-by-field controlled fires.

It was typical for families to surround a field with brooms or shovels; they would then ignite the dead grasses and allow the breeze to spread the flames. As field mice and occasional rats ran out of the burning fields, they would swat and kill them to keep for later to eat and make *sukwar* (their gravy-like stew into which they would dip their *diva*). On occasion, these field fires got out of control and whole villages had their straw roofs burn off their homes. As the heavy burning roof collapsed within, the contents such as clothing and furnishings were also destroyed. There was nothing like fire insurance, so it meant starting over again when that happened.

During the wet season, conversely, it rained nearly every day, but usually only a shower or thunderstorm for an hour or so, after which it would clear and be extremely humid. On rare occasion it rained all day and these were times when low places would flood. During the rainy or wet season everything greened up; fields were planted and garden plots were begun by most of the missionaries.

The orchard workers whom I managed, no longer needed to carry water from the Hawal River to water all the citrus and tropical trees so that I was able to hire fewer men on a week to week basis during the rainy season. The foliage with many native flowers made the landscapes come alive and it was very picturesque. With the humidity very high and the temperatures well past 100, most humans did not work from about 11.30 a.m. until 2:30 or 3 in the afternoon. We started early, had a siesta, and finished later on normal workdays.

BVS Adventures

Brethren Volunteer Service workers on the mission field in Nigeria became a significant complement to the missionaries stationed there during the middle 1950s, when I was there. Of those I specifically remember from 1955 to 1957, there were four of us stationed at Garkida. Besides myself were Curt Weddle, Bob Baker and Elvis Cayford. Elvis and Bob worked in the mission garage caring for mission vehicles, electrical generators and all the equipment needing service and repairs.

Curt was in elementary education and some agriculture work. I worked as Office Administrative Assistant, orchard manager and also taught 5th grade English in the primary school. At the Lassa Mission Station was Earl Dibert who was handyman there in construction, building upkeep, equipment maintenance and repair and general maintenance.

On a visit to Lassa, some 80 miles distant, I spent a couple days of R&R with Earl getting to know him and meeting the missionaries stationed there at that time. They were Irvin and Patty Stern and Dr. Paul Petcher and his wife Pat. John and Mildred Grimley had by then spent a number of years in Lassa teaching and preaching, but had just opened a new mission station at Uba, some twenty miles or so from Lassa on the road back to Mubi. It was at Mubi where H. Stover Kulp was stationed then and was beginning the campus to teach native men and women to become teachers of their own people.

After my short stay with Earl in Lassa we planned to return to Garkida where I was living and where Earl intended to pick up supplies to take back to Lassa. We were traveling on a dirt road between Garkida and Lassa in a Jeep truck chatting away, when the engine began to cut out, then take hold, then cut out again. It behaved as though it was out of gas, or petrol as they said then in this British territory, however we knew we had nearly a full tank of gas. About midway home, the engine coughed and died out in the middle of nowhere. Since it acted like it was not getting fuel, we agreed that there was probably dirt in the gas line or carburetor. It was the middle of the afternoon, we were on a deserted bush road, and we sat for a moment looking at each other and said, "Great What now?"

We quickly analyzed that if there was dirt in the gas line we should unfasten the line and try to blow it out. Fortunately we had a well-equipped toolbox with us so we unscrewed the line at the fuel pump first but could not get close enough to blow back toward the gas tank. We next lay on our backs and slid under the back of the Jeep truck to the gas tank. We were able to unfasten the gas line at the tank but the line was woven through the steel framework of the chassis and we had to bend it downward to get it free.

The gas line was flexible to a point and care needed to be taken not to crimp or break the line. I was holding my finger over the hole in the tank where the gas line was attached and I said to Earl, "The line is designed to be flexible so you should be able to bend it down to clear the frame so you can get your mouth on it to blow through." Earl responded, "It's flexible, but you can only bend it so far" and "SNAP"—it broke off about six inches short of the coupling at the tank. There we lay—on our backs, under the truck, in the roadway, me with my finger on the hole where the line was formerly connected, to keep the gasoline from leaking out and Earl with a short piece of gas line in one hand and a wrench in the other. We looked at each other and both burst out laughing out loud for a couple minutes at our predicament.

We were unsure if any natives were nearby, but we saw nobody, nor would they be of any help if they appeared. No other vehicle had come by nor did we expect any would, the rest of the day. We were not afraid of wild animals; we could sit in the truck cab if anything dangerous came by. My finger was getting numb so Earl crimped the six-inch broken piece and we screwed the coupling back into the tank so that now we had the gasoline secure from leaking all over the ground.

This was before the age of cell phones or any radio contact. Even if another vehicle happened by it was nearly certain they would be of no more help than we were ourselves. It became obvious that we would need to figure this one out ourselves if possible. Since the gas line was loosened at both ends, we figured if we could remove the line without further damage, we might be able to fashion a siphon effect, gravity flow if the gas tank was higher than the carburetor.

We unfastened the gas tank in the rear of the truck, with some difficulty and lowered it to the ground. Then we piled some boxes in the back of the pick up so that we fashioned a platform about equal to the height of the rear window. We lifted the gas tank, which was nearly full, up onto the top of this platform, and secured it there with ropes we had along. Then we took the gas line and carefully fashioned a bend into the filler hole of the gas tank, around the side of the cab and down to the carburetor, which was now lower than the gas tank. We siphoned the gas to get it started and connected the line back to the carburetor leaving the hood partly open. With fingers crossed, Earl jumped into the jeep and after cranking the engine a number of times, it caught and the engine started. We both had to get into the cab through the driver's door since the gas line was wrapped around the passenger side door.

The adventure ended just before it got dark as we pulled into the mission station at Garkida. We surprised both ourselves and many of the missionaries at the station with our ingenuity and were quite proud of ourselves.

CHAPTER 15

SHORT VACATIONS

O n occasions, which were rare, due to distances involved and availability of vehicles and schedules, some of us BVSers were able to plan and get together for fellowship and fun with some adventure thrown in. We learned of a natural wonder, within hiking distance from one of the mission stations, known as Jaffa Falls. Five of us decided to make the hike during the early part of the dry season. Our hope was to get some exercise, photography, sport and fellowship on this one-day excursion. Leaving the mission station soon after breakfast, we hiked some eight miles over sandy, rocky tundra hoping we could find the falls and hoping that there would be water still flowing over the brim or crest of the falls. During the dry season, the stream dried up with only a stagnant pool at the bottom. This pool attracted various forms of wildlife year round since it was the only open water for miles around. Conversely during the height of the rainy season the falls became quite spectacular. The height of the falls is over 100 feet of clear drop into the pool below.

After hiking about an hour or so, with the early sun beating down on us we found a few scraggly trees under which we took a break for a drink from our canteens, and a short rest. Continuing another hour or so we finally came to the rim of the falls and saw a breathtaking scene. Fortunately, for our video benefit, there was still a fairly strong stream flowing over the top creating a mist as it plummeted to the pool below. As we looked down into the pool below, we noted that there were two crocodiles about six or seven feet long, lazily swimming there. Bright colored birds flew nearby and the scene before us was like coming out of the desert into another world. We busily began taking pictures and slides of the beauty of that spot.

We were obviously very hot from walking and the plus 90-degree temperatures that day. One of the guys said, "Boy, would I love to take a dip in that pool down there." It was almost like a dare to a group of young men. We looked at each other and I said, "With crocodiles?" Well, we began to explore our options and the possibilities. We had a high-powered rifle with us and figured that if we posted one of us above guarding the pool, the rest of us might be able to sneak a quick swim. We had not planned to do this when we left camp, but as per usual, we all had on hiking shorts, which we reasoned could easily be used as swim trunks.

The more we looked into the pool and the more we talked about it and the hotter the sun was getting, the more reasonable the plan sounded. Curt volunteered to remain on top as sentry and the rest of us began our hike down the side of the chasm to the pool below. By the time we arrived at the side of the pool below, the crocodiles had disappeared, seeing and hearing us approach. With some trepidation, we stripped to our shorts and prepared to jump or dive in.

The plan was, we would stay near the edge and if any crocodile appeared, Curt would fire a shot to either scare or kill the croc so it would not harm us. Who would go in first? All of us we decided. We jumped into the pool off the rocks below the falls, splashed a bit and retreated—just in case. So far so good and was that water ever refreshing. (I digress to explain that due to pollution and river sickness, none of us had been able to take a swim since leaving the states, so this was really a wonderful opportunity.) When we learned that it was deep enough to dive, some of us dived in and we took photos of each other diving in. In retrospect, I suppose all of us were fearful but none of us wanted to appear "chicken," so we continued to frolic believing that our splashing and activity would frighten away the crocodiles.

After about 15 to 20 minutes of this enjoyable and refreshing activity, at a time when all of us were in the water, a rifle shot rang out and splashed into the water not 20 feet away. Never have three guys, in the history of mankind, gotten out of the water as fast as we did. Not seeing any crocodile or imminent danger, we looked up at Curt who was bent over in laughter. He had not seen either crocodile, but just wanted to give us a scare. He succeeded. We decided we had enough swimming for the day, and were sorely tempted to scurry back up to the brim, grab Curt and throw him down to the crocs, but of course we were all pacifists and he had the rifle.

During the second year of our stint on the Nigerian mission field, the opportunity arose for Bob Baker, one of our fellow BVSers, to transfer and relocate from Waka to Garkida. Since Curt and I had room to spare, it was decided that Bob would join us in our home. He worked mostly in the automotive shop with Herb Michael, a missionary, and Elvis Cayford another BVSer. During that time the three of us planned and decided to take a vacation we had earned, on motorcycles. We each borrowed a cycle from one of the missionaries on station and planned a trip into a neighboring country of West Africa called, at that time, the French Cameroons. We filled up with gas, packed a change of clothes, filled our canteens with water and left Garkida early in the morning for our roughly 100-mile trip to the border of the

Cameroons. Along the way we traveled mostly on dirt roads and for some stretches on sandy footpaths through villages.

We got into areas where motorcycles rarely if ever had traveled and natives rushed from huts to ogle and sometimes wave at three white men speeding by. Dogs were a constant hazard, especially if driving too slowly. They would bite at your legs and ankles as they ran alongside. At the same time, it was difficult to drive fast when you were on paths of loose sand for fear of wiping out. When on these paths, the three of us would space ourselves about 200 feet apart to avoid each other's dust.

On one occasion, when riding a narrow path, I was third or last of the three of us riding about 200 feet behind Bob when I noticed a large dog had raced out to bark and bite at Curt, who was in the lead. He was kicking and feeding gas and fishtailing as he tried to speed up. Soon the dog gave up and saw Bob coming. The dog proceeded to try the same thing with Bob with similar results. I figured I was next and was accelerating all the time so that by the time I got abreast of the dog and it began coming at me, I merely held out my foot (wearing 18" combat style leather shoes). The shoe caught the dog up alongside the head, sending him tumbling. All I felt was a thump and all I heard was a yelp. I don't suppose that dog was eager to chase another cycle rider for a long time thereafter.

We came to a stream flowing across the path we were on and there was no bridge. The water running across the drift was muddy and we could not tell how deep the water was or whether our cycles could get through without drowning out. Bob and Curt suggested that since I had the biggest and highest cycle, I should try driving through first so they could see how deep the water was. I was outvoted and, with some trepidation, I put my feet on the handlebars and drove slowly through. We were lucky the water was only about 18 inches deep and we could all ford the stream without getting wet.

Finally around noon we got to the border between Nigeria and the French Cameroons. We stopped to take pictures at the sign along the narrow single lane dirt road, which indicated the border. We found this a unique experience in that we would now change from driving on the left side of the road as we did in Nigeria to the right side as we always did in the States. It is somewhat difficult to immediately switch from one mode to the other since reactions to many traffic situations become ingrained and automatic.

If you can visualize, for instance, traveling on a narrow road and meeting another vehicle at the crest of a hill or around a curve, tendency is to automatically dart to the right to avoid an accident. Wrong!! In Nigeria, you swerve to the left instead. Many severe accidents occurred over the years—some with injury to missionaries—while traveling the roads of Nigeria. There were some instances where two missionaries met on the road in similar circumstances, *both* made the wrong (right turn) decision and avoided each other. Lucky break. In any event, we now had to put into play the traffic rules we use in the States so long as we were driving in the Cameroons where the right side was the right side.

Not long thereafter, we came to the town of Garowa and for the first time on our trip we were treated to some paved roads, for just a few miles in and around the town. I was briefly separated from Curt and Bob for a few meters and during this time, a policeman saw me coming down the street. He stepped out into the street and waved me over to stop. I did so. I knew I had not been speeding and could not understand why he was pulling me over. He began speaking in French. I held up my hand and said, "I do not understand French, and can you speak English?" He then said, "I wish to see your particulars." I wasn't sure what my "particulars" were but I fished out my Nigerian driver's license and handed this to him.

He looked at it, gave it back to me and asked for my "insurance papers." I said, "I don't know what you mean by insurance papers." With some difficulty, he finally helped me to understand that to drive in their country I must have papers showing my vehicle is properly insured. I explained that I only borrowed the cycle from a friend for a vacation trip and didn't know anything about such papers. The officer issued me a ticket and summons to appear in court with papers.

To make a long story short, I notified Charlie Bieber when I returned that he forgot to give me the insurance papers for the motorcycle to take along on our trip. He said he never heard of such a thing. I went to Yola, the northeast capital city of Nigeria, had a hearing, explained the situation, was told by the judge that ignorance of the law is not an excuse, and had my driver's license lifted for one year. I paid a fine and returned to the bush in Garkida. We all had a laugh since no officer of the law had ever been known to visit Garkida and whether I had a license or not was of no consequence to driving to the various mission stations. It did cause a bit of disappointment to the overall cycle trip however, to have to end in such a way.

CHAPTER 16

LEPROSY

Not more than a mile or two from our home base in Garkida, where I was teaching and working in the central headquarters office, was a small village called Virigwi. In that entire region, Virigwi was noted as the location of "the Leprosarium," a community of lepers surrounding a hospital where they were treated. The location was isolated to a degree due to the infectious nature of the disease. The Church of the Brethren Mission incorporated and included this program of care and treatment by supplying doctors and nurses and equipment to the cause. Aligned with the mission's staffing, the British influence was felt in that they were still, at the time, the official government authority in Nigeria and the hospital became an invaluable asset in northern Nigeria and the whole country learned of its successes.

The reputation and success of the Leprosarium at Virigwi was due primarily to the work and study of Dr. Roy Pfaltzgraff, a Pennsylvania native, who with his wife Violet, spent many years working with these unfortunate victims. Along with Dr. Pfaltzgraff during those early years, there were various nurses who worked hand in hand with him to effect cures and treatment over long periods of time. The reputation of the good success of their program spread and patients arrived from distant places to receive care.

Dr. Pfaltzgraff submersed himself into this age-old problem of caring for lepers to a point where it became a personal thing with him. He studied all the aspects of the disease—how it was contracted, how it could be treated, what areas of the world has already had some success in treatment, what medications would be needed and how to obtain them, what facilities would be required to quarantine patients from each other or those susceptible, who would pay for care and a myriad of difficult and unanswered questions. His determination became almost an obsession—to the eventual benefit of hundreds of lepers.

As a boy going to church and Sunday school, I heard about lepers and missionaries and saw pictures of victims who had lost fingers, toes or even arms and legs. I assumed that if I were to visit an area where leprosy abounds, I might find fingers or toes lying around if I searched hard enough. I was therefore, surprised and intrigued to learn that these various digits and limbs did not fall off, but unless amputated surgically, were retracted into the larger limb or body as the bone structure and tissue supporting them deteriorated.

One of the curious symptoms of leprosy is the loss of feeling in the extremities. If one has no feeling in the feet, for example, one could stand at one spot for hours at a time without moving or shifting weight. This would cause loss of valuable blood circulation leading to sores. The sores became infected—walking barefoot or with dirty bandages—and eventually require amputation. A finger or toe might be fractured from a fall or kicking a barefoot toe into a rock. The leper feels no pain so continues to walk on the foot or use the finger unknowingly until the bone deteriorates and the tissue retracts into the hand or foot. It is common to see a leper with no fingers on a hand but upon close examination, note that evidence of a fingernail can be seen on the stump where once the digit was located.

Another common effect of long-term leprosy is the loss of cartilage in the nose so that unsightly nasal passages are open to frontal view. For the most part, the disease includes little pain due again to the fact that there is loss of feeling. First evidences are usually with skin eruptions and blotches on various areas of the body. This disease is especially contagious to children, but not so much to adults except over a long period of time.

The good news is that the disease is successfully treatable over a long period of time. The bad news is that too many of the patients remain at large until the disease has progressed to a deforming point before choosing to go to the hospitals where treatment can be found. They also expose other family members to the danger of infection. Current times are much better with information, treatment and isolation. Back in the 1950s, however, too many waited too long before seeking treatment which was available to them.

The risks and the dedication of medical missionaries such as the Pfaltzgraffs were truly remarkable. He was very humble by nature, so that few learned of Roy's knowledge, success and expertise in the field of treating leprosy. He was a pioneer in many aspects of the disease and its treatment and only decades later became known for his sacrifices and commitment. His efforts and dedication saved scores of lives and brought comfort and healing to literally hundreds of Nigerians. His research on the subject also became helpful in other countries where leprosy was prevalent.

As mentioned, the Leprosarium, and the Pfaltzgraff residence were located about 1 ½ miles from Garkida and the general hospital there. For a period of a few months during my stay there, the missionary physician, Dr. Marvin Blough and his family, went back to the States for their furlough and the Garkida Hospital was without a physician. During that time, Dr. Pfaltzgraff was required to do double duty. He did his rounds at the Leprosarium and then came in to the hospital to take care of emergencies and patients there. My part of this arrangement was to be available to "go fetch the doctor" during the night if an emergency arose.

One of the native nurse aides would pedal his bicycle to our home on campus and knock on our door arousing me from sleep. He told me they needed the doctor at the hospital. I would throw on a shirt and shorts, jump on the motorcycle, and race down the road to notify Dr. Pfaltzgraff that he was needed. He in turn would quickly dress, get into his jeep, and race to the hospital to treat the patient.

On one such occasion I recall, it had been raining earlier that evening and many puddles of water remained on the roadway. It was the coldest time of the year when night temperatures fell to the 50s. At 50 miles per hour with one small headlight, the puddles were impossible to avoid. I remember getting very wet and muddy on that trip and worst of all being wet and riding fast in 50-degree weather, I got as chilly as any time during the two years there. I was freezing in fact, since our bodies were accustomed to much warmer temperatures—but the effort was successful as the doctor saved another life.

Digging a grave. One man is down in the hole scooping out a seating place for the deceased.

Women going fishing.

A typical compound of natives.

A typical Christian Bura family ready for church in front of their guinea corn harvest.

Burning off fields at the end of dry season.

The new Garkida Church built in 1956 during our stay.

Ten-feet tall guinea corn (sorghum).

CHAPTER *17*

ADVENTURE TO CHIBUK

About a year after arriving at our mission station, it was brought to my attention that, since Garkida was the central administrative and supply point of all our mission stations, a trip was necessary to get supplies to some of the outlying stations. I was asked if I would be interested in driving the lorry from Garkida to Lassa, then on to Chibuk and finally by dry season road, back to Garkida. This route would be approximately 100 miles. The truck was a 15-ton, stake body and had the driver's steering wheel on the right side (since we drove on the left). It took a while to get used to the gas pedal up against the right side panel and the gearshift to operate with the left hand instead of the right, which was how I had been accustomed when driving similar trucks in the States.

I do not remember who it was that accompanied me on that trip, but I believe it was either Curt Weddle or Bob Baker, probably Bob. Anyway, we were two BVSers who were entrusted with the truck and its load of freight. I did all the driving, having had some experience with similar vehicles. We were warned that on the road from Lassa to Chibuk, there was one area that was swampy and the road got slick sometimes when it had recently rained. Everything was going quite well; we had already visited Lassa, unloaded some crates there and said our farewells.

While traveling along, Bob and I were talking about various experiences while in Africa. We were traveling only about 30 miles per hour, since we were on dry season road and it was a tight one-lane width. If any other vehicle approached, we would need to get off on the shoulder of the road to pass. Dry season road meant that the roadway was subject to being washed away at low spots after the rains began and it would basically be impassable until the end of the rains each season, then rebuilt at those low streams areas. Therefore it was assured that it would only be passable about 6 months per year. We were making the trip at the beginning of the rainy season, but believed we could get through before the washouts.

As we were going around a gentle curve to the right, I made a comment that "this might be the place we were warned about that got slippery sometimes." I had no sooner said the words than I felt the back end of the truck coming around and we began to slide sideways off the road. Because we were not going fast I was able to avoid a couple trees and bring the truck to a stop about 20 feet off the roadway. The engine had stalled, so I started it again and found that I had no traction. Even though we had dual wheels in the back we just sat and spun the wheels.

Not wanting to get into the mud any deeper, I cut the engine and we got out to see what we were going to do. We were really in the bush with nothing visible except scrub bushes and a few small trees. We were miles from either of the mission stations with no known native villages nearby. We decided to chop down some bushes and wedge them under the back wheels. We had one small hatchet and one shovel in the back. As we were chopping brush, a native appeared out of nowhere. He did not speak either English or Bura so we conversed in sign language. It was pretty obvious to him what was needed so he helped put branches in the path of wheels as well. Soon another native man appeared, then another and another. Within 20 minutes there were about a dozen men and boys gathered around the truck. We now had laid a good amount of debris under the wheels and up to the road surface. I motioned all of them to get behind the truck and push as I started the engine and slowly engaged the clutch. We did some wheel spinning, but the truck began to move a bit and soon we were back on the road surface.

I got back out of the truck to thank them. I had nothing to give them. I thought about a ten shilling note I had in my wallet or a few shilling coins in my pocket, but immediately knew I would need to give each of them the same gift or I was in trouble. Therefore, I instinctively reached out my hand to shake theirs and every one of them came forward to shake my hand and bow slightly. I then waved, got back into the truck and we drove away, thanking the Lord for His providential care over us.

We proceeded on to Chibuk without further incident and arrived late in the day. This was one of the most remote stations at that time and pretty much isolated 6 months of the year because of the roads as mentioned. The missionary couple at that time was Gerry Neher and his wife and the nurse on station was Iris Neff, R.N., a single lady. They were joyous to see us and we had a good time in fellowship for two days with them.

As a diversion the next day, Gerry, Bob and I went on a short hunt looking for wild game in the area. The only desirable game we found was a Thompson's Gazelle. This game animal is one of the most fleet afoot in the entire world. I heard Gerry who was to my left about 50 yards holler, "Coming down," meaning something was coming my way, I heard the rifle retort from Gerry's 30-06, then I raised my rifle, clicked off the safety and paused—however nothing appeared.

I inched forward slowly in case whatever was coming was hiding or wounded. Soon I heard a low gurgle ahead and found the gazelle under a bush breathing its last breath. Gerry had made a good shot and there would be some good meat for a couple weeks for them. He told me later that the gazelle was already running at full speed when he squeezed off his shot. I was impressed how he had made a fatal shot on a very small target running at 50 MPH from left to right while freestanding.

We were eager to continue and conclude our trip, mostly because, as mentioned, the rains had already begun and a long stretch of questionable road lay ahead. There was only one place where we might have major problems if the seasonal drift had been washed away. The other low spots could likely be forded with a truck our size. When we approached this questionable drift, I was shocked to see that much of the drift had already been washed away and was fearful that what was left might not support our truck width and weight.

We stopped, got out, took a close look at the firmness of what was left and at the truck and at each other. I thought it looked like what was left was too narrow for the width of the dual wheels. If we slipped off the edge, the truck might well topple over onto its side because of the steep grade. I suggested we take a piece of rope and measure the width of the truck tires and that of the drift. The result showed that the inside tires could fit but the outside tires would hang over the edges. With Bob standing out in front of the truck, I lined the truck as best I could and approached watching Bob to tell me to steer more right or left. I eased across the drift with the outside duals over the edges and with a prayer or two everything held and we were able to cross successfully. I'm sure the next rain made that road impassable. It was almost as though the rains waited for us to get on with their season, because within twenty-four hours we had another rain. If we had not been able to cross there, we would have needed to return to Chibuk and go back the way we came with no assurances that the road back the other way was passable. You can imagine our relief to be on the home side of the last barrier of our trip. After crossing that last drift, my hands and shoulders were weak and shaky, like after being in an accident.

Upon returning to home base at Garkida, we had some stories to tell and I could sense that the missionaries there were also praying for our safe return and they also were relieved to have their truck and their BVSers back in one piece.

CHAPTER *18*

A STROLL THROUGH THE NORTHERN NIGERIA VILLAGES . . .

anguage has been and I suppose continues to be both a barrier and an interesting phenomenon in the country of Nigeria.
Unlike the United States, where one can travel for thousands of
miles and still be in English-speaking territory, in northern Nigeria, it is typical to walk or drive less than 25 miles and be into another dialect or language area. It has been estimated that in West
Africa alone there exists over 200 different languages or dialects.
It has been difficult to find widespread unity or even getting a
message out to all the people in the country—partly because lack
of good communication tools such as radios, telephones, etc., and
partly because of not understanding the many languages spoken
throughout the areas and countries.

Originally, the Church of the Brethren Mission in northern Nigeria was centered in two language areas, Bura and Margi.
The missionaries in those two areas learned and taught in the
local vernacular. As the mission expanded, other languages or
dialects were encountered. This made the teaching and printing
of languages in their local language more and more difficult and
inefficient. A general language in all of northern Nigeria, understood by most adults was the Hausa language. Therefore, in more

recent times the new workers and missionaries to these same areas are using the Hausa language instead.

Traveling from village to village in the 50s doing evangelistic work, was mostly done for long distances by motorcycle. For shorter distances, it was either walking or bicycle. As a BVSer, we were all encouraged to purchase a bicycle. I bought mine in the city of Jos on the way out to the "bush" the first time and it was delivered by mission truck a few weeks later. It really came in handy for the two years I was working there and, near the time to go back to the States, I sold it to one of the natives for a couple of pounds. He was tickled to get a good bike for so little cost.

We were cautioned early in our stay, not to hand out money or clothes to those we felt needed assistance. The reasoning was that, within minutes, a line would form at your door, and one needed to be careful not to show partiality or favoritism. On rare occasions, I ignored this caution where I felt it was warranted. One morning in March, when the morning temperatures often dropped into the fifties, I looked out our front window and saw one of the students there looking into our house, and he was totally naked. This, in itself, was not unusual, but it was very unusual when it was that cold. I went to my clothing drawer and retrieved a used tee shirt, went out, slipped it over his head and it came down to just above his knees. A perfect fit. He thanked me profusely, and walked off proud as a peacock.

I felt good about my decision and went about my morning chores. About one-half hour later the same boy was outside my door, again naked. My first reaction was, "Right, I know this game; he's looking for another shirt." I recall going outside to him and exclaiming, "Wasinda, where's the shirt I just gave you a little while ago?" Tears jumped from his eyes and rolled down his cheeks as he said, "When I got home, my father saw the tee shirt and took it because it fit him." I gave him another and didn't hear anymore from him. Hopefully, he was allowed to wear that one out.

The message of Christ and what it means to be a Christian was brought to these mission areas in the mid twenties, so that in the fifties when I was there one could recognize the children coming to school and church from Christian families as being quite different from those coming from pagan or Moslem families. Like the young lad with the tee shirt problem, that would almost assuredly not have happened with the family who were churchgoers and Christian.

It was typical, however, whether it be clothes or even meals, that the men ate their food first, then the women and lastly the children. If the children were short-changed, that was tough. It was an obvious reason why there were as many serious sicknesses among the children and high mortality rate among both babies and young children. Once the children got to an age where they could scrounge for themselves, they were much better off.

Argument could also be made that children and adults would have fared better with a more balanced diet. For decades, or perhaps centuries, the main staple was what they called in Bura, *diva*, or the thick porridge made from grinding the heads of the guinea corn or sorghum into flour, mixing with water (often polluted) and served with a dipping sauce which could include almost anything to give flavor and palatability. Even though the missionaries, over a period of decades, tried to introduce fresh fruits and vegetables to their diets, by and large the custom of *diva*, twice a day, continues to feed the majority. The *diva* would generally be squeezed off, using the fingers, from the main bowl, and then dipped into the *sukwar* (a sauce or gravy mix), then into the mouth with the fingers. In many cases, if not most, those eating did not worry about washing the hands first and were also dipping into the same bowl with half a dozen others at the table.

The potential for health problems, as you might imagine, was great.

The stalks of the guinea corn grew to heights of ten feet and were quite sturdy. The natives sometimes used these stalks in making fences around their compounds by weaving them together with shreds of bark or rope made from river cactus fibers. During the dry season when the Hawal River ran dry, these same guinea corn stalks were sometimes used to create a "roadway" across the sandy bottom of the riverbed by laying hundreds of them in the sand and it gave traction for the jeeps and trucks to cross without needing to travel miles to the nearest bridge.

One calm, hot afternoon as I was passing a compound in the village, I noted that a neatly created pile of goat dung was slowly being burned. There was no flame, it merely smoldered away and slowly consumed the pile of manure. I was intrigued and inquisitive, since I had never seen this before, so I asked the woman there why she was doing this. She seemed somewhat embarrassed (I never could tell if these very black people were blushing or not), but she told me that she waited for a day with no wind like that day. She burned the pile of dung which she had saved in a corner of the compound and after it was all consumed, she would carefully scoop the ashes and sift them, obtaining from the ashes salt, which she could use in her cooking. I wasn't planning to eat there anyhow. It just caused me to marvel at what lengths and with what ingenuity mankind could employ to survive and even enhance their simple lives—especially when the price of iodized salt was relatively small.

CHAPTER 19

THE JOURNEY CONTINUES (AGAIN) . . .

In the distance, I was hearing the beat of drums during the middle of the day. This was unusual, since most of the neighborhood would be working, going to school, or attending to daily chores. It could only mean one thing, I concluded. Someone had died and the family was both notifying the larger community of the death and grieving that death with their traditional dance of death. The mother or the wife of the deceased would paint her legs dark red from the knees down to the feet, take up a wooden rod about four or five feet long and chant as she marched around the compound where the body lay. If the mother herself were the deceased, then the husband or father would take up the dancing ritual. All the while, the drums would beat, sometimes for hours. The dancing ritual was done to "drive away the evil spirits."

During this interval, the men would gather at the burial place and begin digging the grave. The whole process needed to be done within 24 hours since there was no opportunity to embalm and, with the heat, the decay process would be swift in coming. What intrigued me most was the way in which the grave was dug and prepared. First of all a circular area about six to eight feet in diameter was dug to a depth of about two feet. Then in the very center of this circular depression another hole was formed only about 20 inches in diameter—depending upon the girth of the deceased.

This hole was dug down to about four feet and then a hollowing out beneath where the dirt was scooped out to form a tiny room. This area was shaped with a step like a seat. The deceased was wrapped and dressed with clothing as though they were still living, let down through the 20-inch hole and placed in a sitting up position. Finally, boards were laid over the hole and the eight-foot circular depression was filled in with dirt and leveled off. The process effectively created a tomb with the body sitting in place. I was curious as to why this was done and asked one of the men about it. He said, "We bury the deceased this way so that when and if the evil spirits visit that gravesite, they will see that person sitting up and believe they are still alive and will leave without doing the corpse any harm." As the Christian influence pervaded over the years, this changed to coffins and burials similar to what we practice. The breaking away from centuries of tradition, however, was difficult even for many of the earlier Christians to accept.

One afternoon as I was riding my bicycle from our house toward the marketplace to look for some curios or artifacts, which I had been collecting to bring back to the States, I passed a tree, which unbeknown to me housed a large hornets' nest. I was wearing the usual outfit of shorts and a loose fitting short-sleeved shirt. As I approached the tree I was riding about 10 or 15 miles per hour and was met by a swarm of hornets, which had been stirred up, by something or someone.

They landed on my face, my neck, down the back of my billowing shirt and proceeded to sting me unmercifully. I increased my speed thinking to outrun them and was swatting with a free hand to rid them, almost crashing my bike into the trees along the roadway. I was headed in the direction of the Garkida Hospital so I kept swatting and pedaling right up to the doctor's residence. Dr. Blough thankfully was there and immediately took me into the dispensary and dressed the stings. Lucky not to have any allergy to beestings, I needed only to endure the pain of about 20 stings. A couple days later, I got my revenge when we waited until near dark when the nest was quiet, and then torched the nest with kerosene-soaked torches.

Many were the days when I wished for some good ice cream. Only once during the two years was I able to pig out on quality ice cream. I was invited by Bob Swank to fly with him from Jos to Lagos to pick up his newly shipped car, which had arrived from Germany. It was an Opel, similar to a Chevrolet, and he was interested in someone to share the driving and for company. I eagerly agreed and we planned the trip quickly since he was eager to get his new car before it might get damaged at the docks. Our flight was uneventful and we were able to locate the dock and sign off for the Opel.

While in Lagos, which was the capital city at that time (today the capital is Abuja), we had some free time before leaving for the North the next morning. We spotted a sign indicating ice cream. We each purchased a pint, sat on the curb and proceeded to eat the whole thing. Boy, was that good!! The next morning we set out to return home and had a good trip. There were no rest stops per se in those years but plenty of jungle for seclusion. There were no restaurants but a few natives along the highway selling fresh-picked fruits.

We were getting hungry, so we decided to buy a couple bananas. The vendor was a young fellow and he was eager to make a sale. He sold us a hand of bananas for 3 pence. Can you imagine about a dozen huge bananas, stalk ripened and ready to eat for 3 pence (about 5 cents then)? We each ate one and were full. We had no idea what we might do with the rest of the hand. My recall is that we reached Jos late that day and the fruit was very ripe, but we gave the rest of the bananas to the rest house where we stayed that night. The trip turned out to be a fun adventure breaking the day-to-day monotony.

When thinking about ice cream I am reminded that each of the missionaries had refrigerators in their houses. Until my experience in Nigeria, I did not know that a refrigerator could function by burning kerosene. We had electricity only about four hours each evening, so obviously they could not be electric. Homemade ice cream made in refrigerators is just not my thing. It is palatable but just a tease. I never did quite understand how a fire could generate refrigeration, but trust me, they worked quite well.

Traveling along through the area where the mission stations were located, it was common to see anthills, some of which reached heights of 10 feet. There were soldier ants and what they called "fire ants" as well. Sometimes these ants would come up through the concrete floors of our houses where cracks existed. I saw an anthill inside one of the houses, which was unoccupied for a while, that was at least three feet high. You can imagine how foodstuffs had to be stored and protected to prevent ants from spoiling them.

The missionary houses at Garkida were located on a gentle slope overlooking the Hawal River, which was just about ½ mile west. Some of the most beautiful sunsets in the world happened while looking out over this river valley basin, especially during the rainy season when more clouds were prevalent. During the rainy season the Hawal usually ran to a depth of 4 to 6 feet but was nearly 100-feet wide at some locations.

When the rains would intensify for days at a time, the river would overflow its banks for a few days. When the dry season arrived, the waters would recede to a trickle and sometimes leave the riverbed completely dry. The water table, fortunately, stayed within about 6 to 10 feet from ground level, so that hand-dug wells and holes in the riverbed did not need to go very deep in order to get water during the dry season. Most of the missionary houses were constructed so that roof water from rains funneled into a large storage tank and could be used for bathing and washing.

All drinking water had to be boiled and then run through a filter unit before it would be safe to drink. Before I began the trip to Nigeria, I had written a letter to Charles Bieber asking about conditions and clothing to bring, etc. One question I asked was whether they had running water. His response received some weeks later, due to the snail mail at that time, was as follows: "We do have running water. What you do is take a bucket down to the river, fill it and run back with it." And I was going to have to work with this guy?

The orchard, which I was responsible to manage, was next to the river. One day, while tending to chores in the orchard, I heard a lot of excitable chatter coming from up the path. I turned to see a column of native women heading toward the river with their fishing nets. What a sight!! You see, their fishing nets were circular and about 10 feet in diameter. They were composed of a large wooden circular frame made of tree branches with netting stretched over the frame. They carried these nets by putting the center of the nets on their heads like huge hats and walking to the river to fish. This was a fun activity for these women who always went as a group and fished at the same spot.

Their time together was obviously social in that you could hear their laughing and cackling from quite a distance. Two of them would lower one net, then stand on it while it rested on the bottom and continue their talking and laughing. Soon, they would reach down and both lift up the net in a swift motion. Often they would have caught a couple small fish six inches or less. They would pop the fish into a bowl they had balanced on the tops of their heads, place a lid on the pot and commence to lower their nets again for another try.

Most times, there would be about twenty nets working within talking distances with two women on each net. What really amused me, as I watched, was that on occasion one of the nets would come up with a real "keeper" of about 12 inches in the net. Then there would be screaming and shouting like you would not believe. Following such a catch, all the other women would move toward that spot and quickly let their nets down. I presume they figured all the big ones were at the same spot. In the States you have your quilting parties and women's clubs—in Nigeria your fishing parties. Gossiping needs to be perpetuated I suppose but more important, the socializing.

Two-room schoolhouse we built with help from back home.

The new school with first students and teachers, 1957.

Burning goat manure. The ashes are then sifted to obtain salt used in cooking.

Whenever there is a chance for a ride, there's no lack for riders.

CHAPTER 20

OBSERVATIONS, IMPRESSIONS, ETC . . .

When reviewing an experience of two plus years in a place like northern Nigeria, not all is adventure—not all is special—there are always some negatives, just as in any life experience. Sometimes I was asked, "What did you do for fun?" Fun is different based on personality, likes and dislikes. For me, a single man aged 20 to 22 I learned quickly that there was very little social life, at least with any girls my own age. It is obviously an age when one thinks a lot about relationships and dating the opposite sex. Already mentioned in foregoing chapters, a few opportunities arose to share times with some of the fellows my own age, also in BVS, but there were no young women assigned there. The only females our own ages were the native girls. The culture, educational levels, language, and even the hygiene of those prospects, however, never caused any of us fellows even remotely, to consider close relationships.

There were no "places" where social activities existed. The only evening activities after the workday chores were completed, were Sunday night and Wednesday night church services. Most of these were attended to show support for the missionary efforts of that day, and much of those services were not understood due to language barriers. The singing was very spirited and the tunes were familiar as being the same tunes to the hymns we sang in the States, only with different language lyrics. Sometimes, during the evenings, we would gather at one of the missionary's homes to play cards or table games.

In most cases these missionaries had their own families and the age compatibility was not there. What did consume most of our time, therefore, was letter writing or journal writing to all our friends back home. I corresponded weekly to my parents, to the Sunday School at our congregation (incidentally, my Sunday School letters were read to the entire Sunday School each week), to about five or six girls back home that I had dated and with whom I decided to keep up a relationship, and to various other friends and relatives.

I wore out numerous pens and sent hundreds of mail-grams. I was fortunate to have most all of these persons reciprocate and anxiously looked forward to the weekly mail *lorry* (truck). One of the problems with these kinds of writing relationships is the chance of being misunderstood—especially if you tried to kid someone about something. It took about two weeks minimum to get a letter to friends at home and a similar time to receive a response. Therefore if there was a misunderstanding, it took about six weeks to try to get it rectified. Due mostly to this negative aspect of our experience we found ourselves counting the days until we could get back home.

For me this was the most difficult part of my service there. No chance to speak with or hug your parents or siblings or your friends and relatives for two plus years. The missionaries with whom we worked were all really cooperative and nice, so that did cushion this need to some extent, but it was still the most difficult part of serving abroad in a primitive area.

Once each year, all the missionaries who could, converged on the mission station at Garkida for their own Annual Conference. This was similar to the National Annual Conference of the denomination, which we experience in the States. Between the Garkida campus and the Leprosarium campus a mile or two distant, there were about 10 or 11 houses or half of double houses ready for the onslaught of mission workers for the conference.

Each of us tried to house one other family for the occasion, which lasted a couple days. It was a festive time as well as a time of work. I was asked to take the minutes of the meetings during my time there, so that I was busily writing the entire time of the sessions. The new minutes were subsequently produced in our office under Charlie's supervision and appended to the new annual conference booklets we did as my first project in the office.

I would like to share just a word about the living quarters of the average native family where we worked and taught. Each of the families lived in a compound. These compounds were different in size based on size of family and affluence. The typical compound was encompassed within a fence, which was made either of mud and mud block walls or a wall made of hundreds of guinea corn stalks woven together and tied to posts. These walls were about five to six feet high and usually had only one entry/exit door or opening. Within the enclosure would be various (usually round) mud huts with straw thatch roofs. One would be for the father, one for the mother and small children and perhaps another for additional children.

There would be a large mud and straw granary standing five feet tall and about three of four feet around to house their harvest of guinea corn for the dry season food stores. There would be a few small pens or pet houses for chickens, goats or dogs. A pile of firewood would supply fire for cooking or keeping warm during the colder months. Only the more affluent had beds or any kind. Most had rollout mats they put on the ground floor inside their huts and slept on them. It was customary that these compounds would be built in close proximity to each other so that wandering animals and children might be difficult to know where they belong.

It was interesting to me to learn that the building of a new two-room school including the stools, benches and blackboards could be completed for about $500. The second dry season I was there it became necessary to expand, with such a school on the other side of the river. I wrote home and challenged the folks at home and the church to contribute to the new school and also requested my parents to withdraw some of my savings out of my savings account at home.

By the time the new foundations were being dug I was pleased to have in hand the entire $500.00 to build the new school. It was a lot of fun to watch and help in this endeavor. Forms were made about 12 x 12 inches and about 4 inches thick. Mud was mixed with straw, slopped into the forms and patted down firmly. Then the forms were placed on the ground near the school site and lifted up leaving the new brick in place under the hot sun. These bricks were left to bake a few days in the sun and finally used as we would use bricks, to build the walls of the new school.

The new school had an office in the middle space and a classroom on each end, forming a large rectangle. When the walls reached eight feet tall, timber from the palm trees were cut and split for the roof rafters. Literally, tons of straw were cut with sickles and woven into a new roof which when finished was about ten inches thick and quite waterproof. The whole project was completed within 30 days and ready for the next school term. It was a good feeling to have a personal part in building a new school for the students.

CHAPTER 21

THE MUSLIM INFLUENCE...

T he Church of the Brethren Mission Field in northern Nigeria is located in an area, which has become a hotbed of rebellion in recent years. Some of the actions of the Muslim natives have resulted in the deaths of Christians and have destroyed many church buildings. In addition to the threat from religious factions, chiefly the Muslims, there are also urban problems with youth groups forming terrorist gangs. These gangs have torched both Christian churches and the mosques of Muslims. Also, many clergy and other persons have been murdered in these rebellions.

In the mid-fifties, the time period of this book's story, the Christians and the Muslims co-existed in relative peace and harmony. In fact, I am reminded of one rather close friend I made while living in Garkida in 1956. I will omit his name, although it is unlikely that he is still living or might be one of those causing problems today. I will call him Malam. Malam was a Muslim man in his early twenties, about the same age I was at that time. He often wanted to know about the country I came from—the United States.

We shared stories about families and it was my opportunity to share with him my reason for being there. I told him that I was influenced by the life of Jesus and wanted to come to his country to help the people. Malam informed me that he was soon to "take a wife" as they would say in their language. For him it would be his first wife although many of the Muslim men had multiple wives. I told him that for me ever to take more than one wife would be a sin against my religion and against what Jesus taught. I do not know if this ever had an impact on him since I returned to the States at the end of that year. At that time Malam had just the one wife. Not long after he was married, he invited me to come to the compound he had built to meet and greet his new wife.

This invitation was unusual and to me it represented a privilege and honor few Christian missionaries would have had extended to them. I accepted, and we took our bicycles to the site of his brand new compound. It was a small compound, by comparison but then again, his family was just the two of them at that time. We entered a doorway, which was the first doorway in a maze-like circle. We walked in a narrow circular walkway about 90 degrees, then entered another doorway, going the other way about 180 degrees until we reached a third doorway into an open area only about 25 feet in diameter. In the center of the area was a single round mud hut with a thatched straw roof.

This hut was about eight to ten feet in diameter. Everything was so new that the straw was still a golden yellow and the pathways into the center were finely swept with no hint of grass or weeds. I asked Malam if his new wife understood any English and he replied, "Raka, raka" which meant "Just a little bit." We stood in front of the doorway to the hut and Malam spoke a greeting and invitation for his wife to come out. A few seconds later a young lady appeared, totally wrapped in a cloth from head to foot. The only things visible were her eyes looking at me through a slit in the cloth.

Malam introduced me to her and I greeted her in Bura and also English wishing her and her husband health and a long life together. I wished them to have children and be happy. She bowed at the waist, but said nothing. Malam thanked me for coming and seemed very proud that I came and that he could introduce his wife. It was a strange feeling to me because I never heard her voice and all I could see were eyes. It was significant that he considered me enough of a friend to extend the invitation and it was a chance to visit and witness at the same time.

Time was dwindling to an end for the completion of my term of service in Nigeria. It was fun to sell my bicycle and clothes, which were excessive to bring back home. We had a mini auction for two reasons. To try to give these things away would certainly slight some of the students who had become our friends since we could not give equally to all who were interested. Secondly, the schoolboys wanted very much to have some of our clothes, shoes and other items like pens, stationery, etc. Therefore, for a few pennies or shillings, we auctioned off the goods and then turned in the funds to the church offering.

By the end of the two years, I had accumulated quite a variety of curios and artifacts from the culture there which I wanted to take back to show the family and friends. These I crated into a large wooden box and had them sent by boat. Fortunately they did arrive in good condition about two months after I flew back.

Just for fun, I arranged with my older brother Joe, who lived in Vermont at that time, to meet me at the airport in New York upon my return and drive me to our home near Philadelphia. I had informed my parents that within a few weeks I would be in touch with them to let them know when and where I would be coming home. Having my brother and family pick me up and drive me home would hopefully surprise my parents. It was also a way to get Joe and his family to visit for a couple days.

As luck would have it, everything worked out well and we were almost back home when I began to become excited to see my parents and siblings again. We had no furlough or opportunity to even hear their voices for more than two years. When we drove into the lane of my folks' home, mother was outside hanging up the laundry. I was the first to jump out of the car and run up to mom and say, "Surprise!!" For just a second or two she looked into my eyes and I thought she did not know who I was (I had intentionally lost about 25 pounds) but then it clicked and we hugged with that wonderful feeling of being safely home. She then saw the grandchildren and Joe and there was a first-class celebration. I remember her calling my dad at his place of work, just half a mile away, and before long he was also with us. We praised the Lord for His mercy and kindness to us all!!

While the foregoing represents the story of my experience in alternative service, the story does not really end here.

THIRTY-SIX YEARS LATER, I WENT BACK TO SEE HOW THINGS HAD CHANGED AND RAN INTO ANOTHER ADVENTURE. Read the final chapters called "Fast Forward to the 90s."

CHAPTER 22

FAST FORWARDING THROUGH 36 YEARS TO 1994 . . .

A s a result of my alternative service years which began by making the decision to go into Brethren Volunteer Service (BVS) and continued at New Windsor, Baltimore, Bethesda and Nigeria, I returned with a burden on my heart to do something which would benefit those less fortunate than me.

Initially, I returned to the employer I had before going into service, which was a retail hardware store, lumber yard and feed store where my job was sales. I soon became eager to do something more exciting and fulfilling and was hired to manage a retail door-to-door operation in the Lehigh and Northampton Counties of Pa. I had fourteen men under me whom I trained to do retail selling and I was secure in the position and financially very comfortable.

During this interim, I was approached by an officer of a newly-created Board of Directors to serve on the board of a corporation in the early planning stages of establishing a retirement community just three miles from my home. I became excited about this possibility because I felt called to give of my time in service to others and felt that perhaps this was something I should do. During this same period of time I had gotten married to Diane Moyer (yes, I married a Moyer) and we were beginning to have children. In 1962 our daughter Danielle was born and in '64 our son Derek arrived.

This was a busy time since my job involved a 60-mile round trip each day and seldom did I get home before 6 p.m. Many evening meetings were scheduled between obligations at our local Indian Creek Church of the Brethren and the new retirement community project. I was asked to be Vice Chairman of the Board and so elected. The initial chosen name of this endeavor was Peter Becker Memorial Home—named after Peter Becker, the first minister in this country after the denomination moved from Germany in the early 1700s. The gravesite of Elder Becker is located adjacent to the property purchased for the retirement community.

There is a "good news/bad news" story in all of this. The good news was that as things progressed, I was asked to work full time raising funds to build Peter Becker Memorial Home and to subsequently move into the Administrator's role when it was finally opened to receive residents. It was a feeling that this would be an answer to the urgency within me that I needed to be serving others. The bad news; as later I looked back on those decisions, was that I became so involved between my retail management job and planning for the new retirement facility, that I spent far too few hours being a father. In many cases Diane had to be both mother and father, which was not fair to her or to my children.

In the fall of 1968, I resigned my management job and began full time as Director of Development for Peter Becker Memorial Home. My first responsibility was to raise enough of the funds needed to begin construction. During this entire time, from being called to the Board and throughout the planning with architects and financial advisors, the Lord was leading each step of the way. I didn't really realize this was happening, but gave credit to my own skills as a salesperson and motivator. It was not until years later that I sat and considered in retrospect, how each event, crisis, solution, hiring, raising funds, management and decision was the Lord working through me and not my own wisdom or ability. This was and is both a humbling and exhilarating realization and experience. It has been a time of considering how God led me to Nigeria to see the need there and how he sent me back to prepare for His work here.

In 1971, the first resident was admitted into the facilities' "skilled nursing wing." Major additions occurred in 1974, again in 1980, then again in 1990 and since then there has been almost constant change and addition up to this writing in late 2008. At this date, there are almost 500 residents on a campus of 100 acres with more than 200 employees.

The corporate name was changed to Peter Becker Community. Today, it is one of the most respected Continuing Care Retirement Communities in this area.

I was fortunate to be able to lead as Administrator and C.E.O. for 25 plus years until the end of 1993 when I retired. As I approached retirement, I learned about a work camp being scheduled for February of 1994 in Mubi, Nigeria, where a teacher training facility was established. I became excited about the possibility of going back to the areas where I was in my BVS years in the '55-'57 span. The work camp was designed to help erect two housing units for new teacher homes to train for ministry. I signed up and began to prepare to transition from my life's work, into retirement, using the work camp as a buffer.

An important part of preparation was seeing the doctor and getting the shots necessary to avoid tropical sickness and disease problems. I had been seeing a cardiologist prior to retirement because of periods of slight angina pains. I asked about any danger in going for four weeks to Nigeria and, while he did hesitate a bit, he finally said, "Well, you have a leaky mitral valve but have lived with it for years. You have nitroquick tablets if you experience pains; you are taking aspirin to thin blood and your history has been that when you have had angina pain, it has been from overexertion and when you have rested the pain has quickly subsided. Be careful and when and if you feel pain, stop what you are doing and rest a bit and you should be OK."

As the date approached to leave for Nigeria and the work camp, the weather forecast predicted a snow blizzard approaching. Diane and I decided I should travel to Lancaster County a day early, from where we were to leave by van for New York. This we did and I was able to stay in a motel near the meet point the night before. Sure enough, when I got up the next morning, about six inches of snow was already down and it was snowing a couple inches an hour. We managed to leave on schedule and with some difficulty on the thruways and turnpikes; we got to New York in time so as not to miss the plane.

We left New York in the snow and landed in Amsterdam, spent a couple hours in the huge airport, then flew to Nigeria and landed in 100-degree weather. In many ways it was a replay of 36 years ago. In the urban areas I instantly saw much progress in terms of autos, facilities, housing, paving, etc. Even so, it was still 30 years behind current standards in the States. What really surprised me was that the rural areas had hardly changed at all. Homes were still mud block—some with corrugated aluminum roofing, but many still with straw thatch roofing. Few had running water except for a rain collection system they may have used during the rainy season. I couldn't believe it.

When we arrived at our destination in Mubi, we were housed in a dormitory type building with about 20 beds in one large room. The showers were fashioned from a pumping machine, which ran by electricity just an hour or two to fill the tanks above the shower area. The area itself was a series of six three-sided cubicles without doors with a showerhead in each. The water was cold if just pumped but warmer if pumped in the morning and left in the sun all day.

The toilets were unbelievable. Again, a three-sided space of cement block without doors for both men and women. The only thing in the space was a cement slab on the floor with two depressions for the feet and a slot in the concrete about 24 inches long and 4 inches wide between the foot depressions. A bucket of water stood nearby to "flush" the area in case you missed the slot. The procedure was to squat over the slot for either urination or bowel movements. Bring your own toilet paper if you remember. I for one cannot squat for long periods of time, so I did not bring a book along. At least, back in the 50s, we had an outdoor toilet with a seat upon which we could sit, so this represented a regression versus an improvement.

Well, anyway we were not there to complain but to work with the natives and work campers, so we got up early the first day and were shown the area in which we were to work, and had explained to us how, what tools to use, and how we could help. The next day, after orientation, we went to work. First we had breakfast which the native cooks made in a nearby "kitchen area" over outdoor fires with huge pots and pans. I really could not get used to the meals during my time there. Were it not for a few bananas, some homemade peanut butter and a rare helping of chicken, which was usually very tough, I might have soon starved.

The first Sunday, we were driven by jeep to Maiduguri for Sunday church services. In Maiduguri there exists the largest Church of the Brethren in the world. The church building when full seats about 2000 plus those standing at the windows and has two services to accommodate the gatherings each week. It was built on a garbage/trash dump on the outskirts of the city because the Muslims in power in the government there did not want to encourage or assist such a Christian church and would only allow them land on top of the dump.

The Church of the Brethren there took the land, leveled it as best they could and built this large church. Now the city, in some ways, has moved out to them, as many have become Christians there. It was a worship experience I shall never forget to hear that many fellow believers sing, pray and preach for two hours. It may have gone longer, but the next group of worshipers was gathering for the second service that morning.

Only about three days later, during the night at about 2:00 a.m. I got awake because of a severe pain in my chest and left arm. I knew immediately what it was and reached for my nitro glycerin and put one under my tongue. Fifteen minutes later, the pain was no better so I popped another nitro. I was beginning to panic. Everyone else was asleep around me. I remember the doctor's advice, "If you get pain, stop what you are doing and rest until the pain goes away." How do you "rest" from the middle of sleep? I began to notice some lessening of the pain but took a third nitro. It was now 3 a.m. and I was able to sit there, pray and take nitro as needed until the cock crowed—literally. Each morning there the roosters nearby would awaken us sometimes as early as 3 or 4 a.m. if the moon was bright.

When the crew began to awaken around me, I called our Director, Monroe Good, over to my bed and shared with him what had happened during the night. I could tell from his demeanor and his eyes that he was not only concerned but frightened. It was like, "What do we do now? I don't want this guy dying on my watch." I assured him that I was OK, at least for now but I probably should not go to work in the heat. He was quick to suggest that I stay near the bed all day and he would check up on me periodically.

The balance of that day, I felt good without further attacks, but the next day, for about one-half hour I had another attack, which I was able to manage with nitro. The various leaders decided that three of us would drive back to Maiduguri to counsel with a physician who worked in the hospital there. The physician was trained in the States and a member of the Church in Maiduguri. We drove the two hours back to Maiduguri without incident and met the doctor there. He examined me there and proclaimed that the best thing, which could be done, would be to send me back to the States as soon as possible to have an angioplasty done.

We all had return tickets in our possession for the trip back after work camp. We called the airlines about changing my ticket to return on a date as soon as possible. They informed us that they could only do that out of the major airport in Lagos, then the capital of Nigeria, two days hence. We were able to get two seats on a smaller plane flying from Maiduguri to Lagos that same day. We said we would take the tickets and we were off to the airport post haste.

The bigger problem on the horizon now was getting through Lagos safely. It was not a city where white Americans traveled except in emergency. Various Americans simply disappeared in that city never to be heard from again. However, what choice did we have? One of the native church members who had a brother with some influence living in Lagos volunteered to travel with me to assure I was safe and make my connections.

We flew that same afternoon, the four hundred miles to Lagos, with some trepidation. I do not remember the name of the man who accompanied me, but I could sense that he was quite frightened about what might happen in Lagos. When we landed, he was able to contact his brother at his office and update him on the predicament. The brother sent a car to pick us up and took us to his office. From his office I was able to call Diane in the States and inform her what was happening and that I was on my way home.

I told her that in two days I should be in New York at the airport at four in the afternoon and could someone come up and pick me up? I remember her hesitation—first, shocked that I was having heart problems, and second because a second blizzard was beginning in the northeastern U.S. She said, "I'm not even sure we will be able to make it down to the airport in Philadelphia, but certainly not to New York. Could you possibly arrange to get a flight from New York to Philadelphia?" I said I would try and that I would try to keep in touch if anything further happened, but certainly when I landed in New York I would call.

We left the offices of my guardian's brother and I could tell that my guardian was very ill at ease. Also, I was beginning to have another attack. When he saw me fumble for a nitro, he asked me what was wrong. When I told him, he really lost it. He was sweating and looking around as though trouble was about to happen. Now I was getting scared. I asked him if he knew where the American Embassy was located. He said he did and that it was not far from our location. By now I had some real pain which was tough to hide but I gutted through it. I asked him to try to get me to the embassy and I could manage from there.

I saw instant relief on his face and he drove me there without incident and dropped me off. I went in, told them my story and asked for protection and lodging if they had accommodations. They took me upstairs and low and behold, there was a small apartment with running water, a couple beds and all the comforts of home, which I had not seen since leaving the motel in the States. I was able to rest until the next day when my flight was scheduled. I could even order a cheeseburger and fries so I did, since I hadn't eaten much for the past 24 hours.

The next problem presenting itself was how to get safely to and through the airport in Lagos. The embassy promised me that two hours prior to flight they would take me by armored car to the airport and try to arrange safe passage through customs and gates. We left in a Chevy Suburban, which they told me was bullet proof and had phone and radio communications. Partway to the airport, we encountered a group of natives walking in the road who did not wish to move over and let us pass. In fact, when they saw the color of my skin, they began to rock the vehicle for a while.

The driver began moving slowly even pushing some of the mob slightly, with the bumper of the suburban. He was on his phone to the airport notifying them that he would be arriving in about ten minutes at a secure entrance. When we finally got to the airport, the moment we stopped a guard appeared on either side of our vehicle. I was let out with my bag and asked to walk between them through the airport. During that walk I can remember looking at the many people crowded in the airport and I did not see even one friendly face. Each person looked like they wanted a piece of me. The guard told me that if we could get to the gate for boarding, I would be safe until flight takeoff.

I felt like saying, "I surely hope you know what you are talking about," because at that time I did not feel safe at all. We proceeded to the gate listed, my ticket was punched and I was instructed to wait in a well-guarded area where I finally was away from the mobs and felt safe.

From then on, I was on my own. The flight out of West Africa was on time and we flew to Amsterdam in the Netherlands. We would have a three-hour layover, then on to New York. Before reaching Amsterdam, I had another attack of angina pain. I sat upright with a book in hand and tried to refrain from grimacing or showing pain. I was able to get relief in about a half hour, just as we were about to land. I was afraid that if the airline learned of my situation they would not let me fly, so I tried my best to hide it. Ironically, the same scenario presented itself on the flight from Amsterdam to New York. Another spell of heart pain, which I was able to relieve with nitro, happened before landing in New York.

Immediately upon landing in New York, I went to the ticket counter to inquire about a shuttle ticket to Philadelphia. It was the middle of the afternoon and I was lucky to obtain a single to Philadelphia, scheduled to leave about 6 and arriving in Philadelphia about an hour later at 7 p.m. I then called Diane at home, told her I was doing OK and should be coming into Philadelphia around 7 on flight 2110. She said they should be able to make it since the main roads had been plowed and the snow had stopped. What had happened with the weather was that the snows, which happened the day we left New York on our way to Nigeria just 10 days before, had melted, refroze and turned to ice, which at some places was 3 to 4 inches thick. Now another storm had just dumped about eight to ten more inches onto that mess which had snarled traffic between New York and Philadelphia.

My family was able to arrive at the airport in Philadelphia prior to the expected flight, but my flight was now postponed due to backups from the storm. I was supposed to catch the shuttle about 6 p.m. but was told there would be a delay—as yet undetermined. I was concerned that my family would be at the airport in Philadelphia and not know my flight was delayed and begin to worry. I approached the flight desk in New York and had to stand in line for nearly an hour to get to talk with anyone.

I was getting weak and there was no place to sit because the airport was so full of people that every seat was taken and hundreds were standing and sitting on the floor. I finally got to the desk and told them of my concern about notifying my family back in Philadelphia about these delays. They took the flight number and my name and assured me they would notify my family about the delay. I had no cell phone back then and no number to call if I had. After being assured they were on top of everything, I walked outside the terminal for a while to catch some fresh air, it was really stuffy in the waiting areas.

Unbeknown to me, unfortunately, my family was never notified of the delay of my flight and was unable to get any information from the people in Philadelphia. It was as though my flight did not exist. When the delay stretched out for almost four hours to near ten o'clock, I rationalized that although my family would be tired they would be patiently waiting my arrival. They, on the other hand, unable to get any information about my flight became increasingly apprehensive as the hours ticked away. Whom should they try to call? Had I expired or had a heart attack and was I being treated in a trauma room in a hospital somewhere?

When I finally arrived, they were not aware of it until I walked into the waiting area in the terminal where they were all seated. Diane was on the phone with our daughter in Lancaster County sharing the worst-case scenario possibility. My son was impatiently waiting it out hoping for a good outcome. Never have they or I felt relief as at that moment. They now knew I was alive and in reasonably good shape and for me, to be with family in the event I was to have any more angina attacks.

They drove me home for a good night's sleep. The next day I entered the hospital, was examined, sent to Lehigh Valley Hospital in Allentown and after a catheterization was treated with a balloon angioplasty to open an artery within the heart. Good results followed and it would be another ten years until another catheterization was required. I was pleased with the outcome of my adventure but would not recommend it to anyone as a way to travel and see the world.

EPILOGUE

Fourteen years have passed since the medical emergency encountered during the '94 work camp in Nigeria. Diane and I are enjoying our retirement living—now as residents on the campus of Peter Becker Community. We are also enjoying our four grandsons. During the past year the Brethren Volunteer Service Program has held a reunion for all past BVSers. They have also trained and sent out unit #282. (Our unit was #26—just 53 years ago!!!)

My hope is that many more persons and units will come forward, become involved and share their time and talents in the benefit of serving and helping others. The great commission of "Go ye into all the world and teach the gospel" is not just for lifetime missionaries; it is for all Christians whether on foreign soil or close to home. If you accept this challenge, I can promise you that even if you only serve one year or possible two, it will be an experience you will never forget and it will change your life and outlook for the better. Every person has a talent or two. BVS will help you find yours and help you to use it to the Glory of God and your neighbors' good.

I am now 73 years of age and feeling great! Obviously, I got over the emergency of the work camp experience once I got proper treatment. I've also faced another heart concern and had three stints placed into my heart about three years ago. I've been a cancer survivor now for the past 16 years and was diagnosed with macular degeneration ten years ago, which entailed four laser operations and treatments to my right eye. The central vision in that eye is gone but all the peripheral vision remains. That's the negative news.

The positive news is that I am enjoying retirement by golfing and bowling a couple times a week, gardening a 50x50-foot garden with my tiller, writing, reading and traveling internationally and locally and working out in the local YMCA three times each week. I am also active in our local congregation at Indian Creek Church of the Brethren where both my wife and I are deacons. I have been Church Board Chair and Moderator in years past. Diane and I recently returned from a cruise visiting Italy, Croatia, Greece and Spain and enjoying the Mediterranean Sea. I do not share all this to boast but to affirm that God has blessed me and brought me through some difficult experiences. I believe in the power of prayer and also believe that since I am feeling good, He obviously still has work for me to do in His Kingdom here on earth.

Count your blessings and allow Him to work through you in whatever you do and wherever you are. The PURPOSE of each of us on this earth is to PRAISE GOD—it is why we were created. How are you fulfilling your purpose?